Britain's Canals

A Handbook

Nick Corble

TEMPUS

First published 2007
Tempus Publishing Limited
The Mill, Brimscombe Port,
Stroud, Gloucestershire, GL5 2QG

British Library Cataloguing in Publication Data.
A catalogue record for this book is available from the British Library.

ISBN 978 0 7524 4183 2

Typesetting and design by Liz Rudderham
Origination by Tempus Publishing Limited
Printed and bound in Great Britain

Contents

Boaters tend to be social types and enjoy a get together, such as this gathering at Banbury. (Courtesy of Allan Ford)

Introduction

The waterways are a modern success story, an iconic example of the great British talent for re-inventing our past and making it relevant to the present. Who amongst us has not yearned at some point for the chance to indulge in a little bit of 'messing about on the river'? Perhaps being a maritime nation means some kind of affinity with water is in our genes, and as most of us do not live by the sea then the inland waterways are a pretty good substitute.

This book, therefore, is meant for all of us. It celebrates our inland waterways heritage and places it into a modern context. It combines background on how this heritage came about with 'nuts and bolts' information on how to get the best out of it.

In practical terms, this means hard facts and softer guidance on the 'who, what, where, why and how' of the waterways system. It tells you how to get afloat and stay there, as well as where you can go, what to look out for on the way in terms of wildlife, engineering and architecture; how to recognise different types of craft and even, should the fancy take you, how to buy a boat. If you want to go 'whole hog' there are even tips on living aboard. It is, in short, an inland waterways primer.

Its audience goes beyond those who want to experience our canals and rivers by being on them. As part of the Tempus Towpath series, this book is aimed squarely at the full spectrum of waterways users, from those who may simply walk the towpath with their dog to anglers, cyclists, horse riders or the half the population who live within 5 miles of an inland waterway.

It would be impossible to put everything there is to know about the waterways between the covers of a single volume, and different readers will require information on different levels. As such, this particular book has been designed to be easy to dip in and out of, to read a chapter at a time or to use as a reference guide with further sources of information well signposted. Alternatively, you can simply look at the pictures, of which there are many.

So, whether you are already a regular visitor to our inland waterways or intend to become one, whether your acquaintance is long or short lived, or your interest is active or passive, this is the book for you. I hope it manages in its quest to inform, amaze and entertain, and make the world of the waterways accessible to all.

Nick Corble

The Author

Nick Corble announced himself as a canal writer with his first book, *Walking on Water* (Belmont Press), which described a trip down the spine of the waterways system on the eve of the millennium. He followed this up four years later with *James Brindley: The First Canal Builder* (Tempus Publishing).

Subsequent works have included a series of canal-specific guides for Tempus, including *The South Oxford Canal*, *The Grand Union Canal (North)*, *The Grand Union Canal (South)* and *The Kennet & Avon*, as well as contributions to canal and other consumer magazines. Not just a canal writer, Nick has also published a number of walking books and co-authored the definitive history of the fairground attraction the 'Wall of Death' (*Riding the Wall of Death*, Tempus Publishing).

Nick's style is always to make his subject accessible, avoiding jargon and introducing the off-beat to stimulate interest. He is constantly on the lookout for stories of ordinary people who have done extraordinary things. For more on his work visit his website: www.nickcorble.co.uk.

* All photographs are by the author unless otherwise stipulated.

SECTION A

Part of Our History

Today we associate canals with calm and tranquillity, a break from the stresses of modern living, a traditional part of the fabric of our country. It is not easy, therefore, to imagine them as something radical, and quite literally groundbreaking: a source of noise and activity, a threat and at the same time a catalyst for one of the greatest socio-economic changes this country has ever experienced.

After the canals, Britain was never the same again. Whilst canals cannot claim all the credit for this, if indeed credit is due, they can claim a major role. To truly understand our inland waterways it is necessary to gain an appreciation of their roots.

There is no shortage of sources providing a detailed rundown of that history and 'Learn More and Links' provides a list of some of these. In the spirit of being a primer, this book opens with a light skim across the surface of that history until the Second World War: the rise and fall of the canals. The final chapter provides an assessment of what happened next and where the inland waterways stand today. As will become clear, our rivers and canals are literally awash with history, but as also will become clear, it remains a work in progress.

The first period was a time when heroes stepped out of the shadows, monumental structures were conceived and built, and even God was challenged. It also covers disappointment and decline, competition in the face of superior technologies, corporate takeovers and the rise of a colourful subculture. Let us begin.

An important, but easily forgotten, fact is that our waterways system is about more than the canals. For centuries rivers had been used to transport people and goods about the country, with the mouths of different rivers linked by craft capable of passing along the coast. By 1660 there were 685 miles of navigable river in the UK. Later improvements to other rivers, including the Aire in Yorkshire and the Avon, Kennet and Wey in the south, which even had early pound locks built on the same principle that we recognise today, meant that nearly 500 additional miles had been added by 1724.

Where rivers were straightened or their sides cut, they became known as 'navigations' and although they could be seen as precursors to the canals, they remained rivers. Elsewhere channels were cut to bring a river to a particular spot, and these might be seen as closer to a modern canal. The nearest to what we now regard as an artificial waterway was probably the Exeter Canal, a 2-mile stretch alongside the River Exe cut in the sixteenth century. Votes are also cast for the Sankey Brook from St Helens to the Mersey cut in 1757 (later known as the St Helen's Canal). Neither of these, however, were entirely independent of rivers.

Rivers had their limitations. They were subject to the vagaries of both current and floods, whilst most navigable rivers required dangerous flash locks to allow boats to pass natural weirs. Bridges were another hazard. The narrow spans necessary for construction made for significant hazards for any boats passing below.

By the mid-eighteenth century the first rumblings of industrialisation could be heard in the belly of the British economy. People were moving to the towns and the first concentrations of industry were appearing in early factories producing goods such as textiles and silk. However, growth was being stifled through want of a decent transport infrastructure, notably to allow the movement of bulky raw materials and finished products.

The rivers could be made to work but were only any good if one was convenient. The roads were almost as bad, largely because of the lack of a decent means of surfacing them. Muddy, narrow and often rutted, most roads were unreliable and haunted by thieves who were attracted by the slow traffic, and vermin which fed off the food dropped at their sides.

The turnpike system helped but represented an extra cost and could not overcome the basic problem of road transport at the time, namely that loads were limited to the breadth of a mule's back or the size of a cart. Moving coal was a particular problem. Dirty, heavy, awkward and rarely convenient, roads didn't suit the transport of coal and even where there was a river loads had to be broken down and transferred to get them to their final destination.

One town in particular, Manchester, was desperate for a steady supply of the black stuff. Good supplies were available nearby, the challenge was finding a way of transporting it into the heart of the growing metropolis. It was at this point that the fates of three extraordinary characters came together.

One was Francis Egerton, third Duke of Bridgewater, an aristocratic playboy spurned in love who had retreated from London to his estates in Worsley, 20 miles west of Manchester, in the late 1750s. These lands sat on a coal mine which was difficult to exploit partly because the mines kept flooding. Furthermore, whatever they did manage to extract was difficult to transport. The most obvious route into nearby Manchester involved travelling part of the way along the Mersey and Irwell Navigation, one of the country's navigable rivers, the owners of which were happy to take the loads, but at a cost.

Two other men now entered the equation. The first was John Gilbert, the duke's often underrated land agent, who in turn had heard of a man called James Brindley who had gained a reputation for himself in mine drainage. Together (it is unclear who had the idea first), these two men came up with the elegant solution of draining the mine into an artificial waterway which would carry the coal into Manchester – thus solving one problem with another. What made this solution unique was that this waterway would be entirely independent of any river.

Gilbert took control of the mine side of the operation and Brindley the waterway, or canal. The idea of a canal was deemed by many to be preposterous (surely it would leak?), or if not then scandalous (it meant carving through other people's land), and if not this, then blasphemous (who had the right to destroy the divinely inspired land-scape?).

The story of how the canal got built, the struggles to gain Parliamentary approval, to raise the necessary finance and to build the first aqueduct since Roman times, is recounted in *James Brindley: The First Canal Builder*, from Tempus. This records the formative role played by Brindley, not only in the building of the Bridgewater Canal, as the new waterway became known, but also the much longer Trent & Mersey, and how he became the driving force behind the first wave of canal building in this country.

The Trent & Mersey, Brindley's second big canal project, was an alto-gether different proposition. Tellingly, as its name suggests, it was built to link together two of the country's main navigable natural waterways. Most importantly it meant carrying a level surface of water up and over the spine of the country. This required not only locks, a device the Bridgewater notably lacked, but also the determination to not let anything get in the way, necessitating what was probably Brindley's finest achievement – the 2-mile-long Harecastle Tunnel, another first for this remarkable man.

If Brindley engineered the canal, the driving force this time was Josiah Wedgwood, whose story epitomised the economic forces around at the time. Like his fellow potters, Wedgwood was based in the area around Stoke-on-Trent. Whilst there was plenty of demand for their wares from the fledgling middle classes, the landlocked potters could not grow their businesses due to the difficulties of bringing china clay in from Cornwall and getting their finished goods out – the backs of donkeys and rutted roads not being conducive to breakage-free transit.

The Trent & Mersey was the solution, but unlike the Bridgewater no single man had pockets deep enough to finance it. The idea emerged of individuals coming together to fund the project through shares, with 505 shares at £200 each sold to provide the initial working capital, with no individual allowed to own more than 20 shares. A

James Brindley, canal mastermind.

model for funding a renewal of the country's transport infrastructure was born.

Brindley's genius has only recently been given the recognition it deserved. Those close to him when he was alive appreciated his works, but perhaps his great friend and colleague Josiah Wedgwood summed up the view of many when he suggested shortly after Brindley died that he was 'one of the great geniuses who seldom live to see justice done to their singular abilities'.

His skills were manifold. He combined practicality with vision, inventing devices to build his waterways as he went along and in so doing effectively creating a whole branch of civil engineering from scratch. Whilst it is technically true to say he was not the first canal builder, he was first amongst his breed.

Brindley's vision was evident, not only with the Bridgewater and Trent & Mersey canals, but beyond these to a whole system linked together by what he called the Grand Cross. In essence, this was a scheme to link the four great seaports of the day (London, Bristol, Hull and Liverpool) with inland waterways forming a giant 'X', from which branches could be built and the centre of which would lie conveniently close to the coalfields and industry of the Midlands.

Brindley found himself in demand but his days were numbered as he was harbouring an undiagnosed form of diabetes. In a dozen short years he acted as either the chief engineer or a consultant on any new canal scheme going – enough to get things moving but not enough to see them through. The one exception was the Staffordshire & Worcester Canal opened in 1772, and this, along with a section of the Trent & Mersey connecting Stoke with the Trent, meant he saw one arm of his Grand Cross completed before he died. The other arm followed in time with the Oxford and Coventry Canals offering a route to London via the Thames.

Perhaps Brindley's greatest legacy was that he was free with his knowledge and the art of canal building did not die with him. Some of the frenzy did go out of it though, largely as a result of economic difficulties related to the American War of Independence, but things picked up again in the 1790s.

The era known as 'Canal Mania' now followed when almost any scheme could get funding. A period of 'irrational exuberance' followed, not unlike the 'dot com' boom at the end of the last century. During 1793 proposals peaked at twenty-four new schemes, not all of which were built. The economic background remained poor, however, with the fight against Napoleon now proving a drain on both money and the men needed to build the canals.

Despite this, the demand remained. The period from Brindley's first canal to the defeat of Napoleon in 1815 saw a massive shift of the population into the towns and the rise of factories. It also saw continued inventiveness and in 1825 the world's first commercial railway linking Stockton and Darlington was opened – ironically a route originally considered for a canal.

As this mural outside Rickmansworth remembers, living horse power was used for over a century to provide propulsion.

Those with foresight could see that railways represented a threat, although such was the dominance of the canals that it would have been hard to appreciate their strength at the time. The canals continued to thrive in the opening decades of the 1800s, with most companies still paying good dividends through to the 1830s. Money was also still being invested in them with Thomas Telford, the premier engineer of the time, responsible amongst other achievements for the Shropshire Union and Macclesfield Canals, as well as a replacement for Brindley's Harecastle Tunnel which had begun to subside.

The Harecastle Tunnel outside Stoke was an audacious enterprise, both Brindley's original (seen on the left) and Telford's successor (on the right).

SECTION A

TEN CANAL HEROES

James Brindley	Pioneer and inventor of modern canal building. Built the first canal and led the way on the building of aqueducts and digging of tunnels, notably the Harecastle near Stoke. Laid down the basis of the waterways system before his early death
Francis Egerton	Third Duke of Bridgewater, instigated the Bridgewater Canal and by so doing earned the nickname 'the Father of the Canals'
John Gilbert	Unsung hero behind the Bridgewater Canal, the Duke of Bridgewater's land agent who worked alongside Brindley in the cutting of the first canal
William Jessop	Pupil of John Smeaton, perhaps best known for his work on the Grand Junction Canal
John Rennie	Engineer responsible for many of the main canals built through the 1790s, went on to become known primarily for his bridges
Thomas Rolt	Author of *Narrow Boat* and other works which led to the creation of the Inland Waterways Association after the war and the rescue of much of the system from dereliction
John Smeaton	Known as the 'Father of Civil Engineering' who devoted much of his time to canals
Thomas Telford	Probably the greatest of the second generation of canal engineers. Built the second Harecastle Tunnel
Josiah Wedgwood	Vocal advocate for canals in their early years and driving force behind the creation of the Trent & Mersey Canal
Robert Whitworth	Engineer taught by Brindley. Perhaps most famous for the Forth & Clyde, one of the many canals he worked on

If the speed with which canals had grown was impressive, it was nothing compared to the rapidity with which railways usurped them. By 1845 nearly a quarter of the canal companies had sold out to their railway counterparts. In that one year alone more miles of new railways were proposed than all the canals put together. Some of the new railway companies were benign, creating what we would today call integrated transport systems with the canal basins, whilst others were more ruthless, simply buying the canals in order to remove a competitor. In fact, 1845 represented the peak of the inland waterways system with over 4,400 miles of navigable waterway, 3,200 miles of which were part of the connected system.

Just as inspirational as Brindley, Thomas Telford was responsible for many of the later grand projects of the canals.

Something of a polymath with works covering more than simply canals, John Smeaton is sometimes called the 'father of civil engineering'.

The days of high dividends, however, were over. Instead, the canal companies cut their rates and the Government of the day removed some of the restrictions previously placed on them, allowing the companies to raise their own fleets. It was during this time that 'bargees' started to live on their boats along with their families to cut costs, their craft still relying on living horse power for propulsion.

The 1860s saw the introduction of steam tugs and a decade later engines reduced sufficiently in size to fit onto a cargo boat, which could also pull a 'butty' or second, engineless boat in an effort to boost capacity. The canals soldiered on, but by this time the speed and predictability of the railways was self-evident and all they were doing was managing their decline.

The turn of the century brought the diesel engine, but this was a mixed blessing. These were not the machines we know today and needed great skill to operate. Starting them was a performance in itself, requiring a handle and blow torch to warm the thing up. More importantly, the introduction of diesel engines also encouraged the growth of road transport, which before long was even threatening the dominance of the railways. Canals were pushed another notch down the pecking order.

The logistical demands of the First World War provided some reprieve however, and likewise the Second World War, with women in particular coming to the fore in the latter. In between these events, the Great Depression of the 1930s led to a last gasp effort to make the canals more viable, notably with the creation of the Grand Union Canal. This was an amalgamation of seven canals which together had provided a more effective route to London from the Midlands than the original route via Oxford.

A major regeneration scheme was initiated with a widening of the canal from a narrow to a broad basis along much of its length, a process which meant replacing most of the locks. At the same time a Grand Union Canal Carrying Co. was created with its own fleet of boats, but this was to be just another vain attempt to hold back the tide of progress. During this time the River Thames also benefited from a major upgrade

A traditional 'pair' of boats used to double up capacity when the economic squeeze came to the canals. (Courtesy of Allan Ford)

Locks on the Thames were upgraded during the Great Depression and remain in use today.

Worsley Delph, the unpromising point where canals were born.

of its locks. More typically, though, canals silted up from lack of use and became un-navigable. By the end of the war the canals were in a sorry state, their future bleak.

SECTION B

A Network

Old canal hands often refer to 'the system', although to the untrained eye the inland waterways can seem distinctly unsystematic. Look a little closer though and it is possible to see where they are coming from. From its very earliest days the canal system was envisaged by its architect James Brindley as a network. He even had a name for it – the Grand Cross – made up from two roughly diagonal lines linking the four great seaports of London, Liverpool, Hull and Bristol.

The intersection of this cross lay in the industrial heartland of Birmingham and the Black Country. As it happened, Birmingham itself sat on a plateau and as such was avoided by the early canal builders, but the reaction of the great and good of that city epitomised a story that recurred across the country – they built a link to one of the main arteries of 'the system'.

This encapsulates the two initial phases of canal development. The first, completed remarkably quickly and with enormous foresight, was the development of the Grand Cross. This had the double effect of both proving the financial and economic benefits of canals, as well as the technology required to build them and laying down a core for 'the system'.

The second phase began when towns and cities which had originally distanced themselves, quite literally, from having a canal rushed to get involved when they saw the economic benefits of having one. The result was the building of a number of smaller branch lines, or even diversions of the original routes of the first canals, secondary arteries which helped to create the seeming randomness we see today.

To these can be added a third phase, one that combined both tidying up the loose ends of 'the system' and a spate of less rational, speculative building. The initial link with London in particular was far from satisfactory. Initially this had been achieved by the Oxford Canal, with boats obliged to complete the journey to the capital via the Thames. Unfortunately this was a less than reliable route, involving as it did the negotiation of flash locks, which quite literally had to be ridden.

An alternative was required, and was provided by the creation of the Grand Junction Canal from Braunston in Northamptonshire to the

Unsurprisingly, given its position, Birmingham can rightly claim to be at the heart of 'the system', with many rings passing through it.

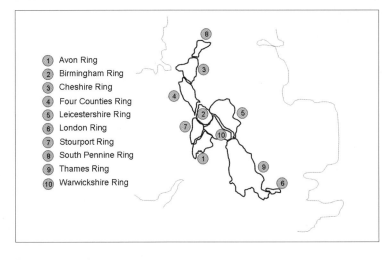

1. Avon Ring
2. Birmingham Ring
3. Cheshire Ring
4. Four Counties Ring
5. Leicestershire Ring
6. London Ring
7. Stourport Ring
8. South Pennine Ring
9. Thames Ring
10. Warwickshire Ring

Top ten waterway rings.

SECTION B

Thames at Brentford, appropriately enough close to the spot where Julius Caesar was said to have first crossed the river. This new canal linked up with the Warwick & Napton and the Warwick & Birmingham Canals to provide a direct link between the country's two largest cities.

At the same time canals were proposed as the solution to all manner of economic ills, some real others imaginary, and such was their popularity that many got sponsored; adding further to the sense of fragmentation, with some canals being built that did not even connect with 'the system'. Most did, however, and for the modern boater this untidiness is part of the charm of the canals. On one level, wandering the system is like negotiating a maze, with lots of dead ends and surprises, whilst on the other there is a wonderful potential to construct routes. With a system over 200 years old it is no surprise that a number of these have become formalised, attracting their own guides, videos and even tea-towels, their popularity reinforced by the fact that hire companies often choose to base themselves at some point on these routes.

Normally known as 'rings' these can involve canals or rivers, the best being a mix of the two. A list of ten of the top rings is provided below.

TOP TEN WATERWAY RINGS

The Avon Ring (109 miles, 129 locks, approx. 60 hours)
Possible to complete in a week if you have an experienced crew, this route takes in stretches of the Avon and Severn rivers as well as the Worcester and Birmingham and North and South Stratford Canals as well as a number of picturesque villages. Other than the rivers, perhaps the highlight of this ring is the opportunity to moor right outside the RSC Theatre in Stratford

Hebden Bridge, one of many highlights on the South Pennine Ring.

The Birmingham Ring (76 miles, 79 locks, approx. 45 hours)

An interesting route taking you through both industrial and rural landscapes and including an opportunity to moor up in the heart of England's Second City and easily completed in a week. The route involves sections of the Birmingham and Fazeley, Coventry, Trent and Mersey and Staffordshire and Worcester Canals, as well as parts of the Birmingham Canal Navigations

The Cheshire Ring (97 miles, 92 locks, approx. 50 hours)

A good 'sampler ring' as it takes in sections of six different waterways: The Macclesfield, Trent and Mersey, Upper and Lower Peak Forest, Rochdale, Ashton and Bridgewater Canals. The Cheshire Ring stretches from the heart of Manchester in the north to as far south as Stoke on Trent taking in large parts of Cheshire in between, hence its name

The Four Counties Ring (110 miles, 94 locks, approx. 55 hours)

This largely rural ring takes in a large section of the Shropshire Union Canal, along with the Trent & Mersey and Staffs and Worcester Canals but needs a full crew due to the locks involved. Key features are the Harecastle Tunnel outside Stoke on Trent, which acts as the main built up area of the ring and 'Heartbreak Hill' through the salt country outside Middlewich. There is also an option to visit the Wedgwood Visitor Centre

The Leicestershire Ring (157 miles, 102 locks, approx. 75 hours)

A long ring, but not over-burdened with locks, this route takes in parts of the North Oxford, Coventry, Trent & Mersey and Leicester

Line off the Grand Union, as well as part of the River Soar. There's staircase locks, five tunnels and long rural stretches to enjoy, as well as some of the brewing centres along the Trent, although you need to allow two weeks to complete the ring

The London Ring (44 miles, 25 locks, approx. 25 hours)
A leisurely route through the north of London and along the Thames utilising the Grand Union Main Line as well as its Paddington and Regent's Park Branches, including passing right by London Zoo. As its name suggests this is an urban route and some planning is required to allow you to select the best places to stop, but with this in mind there is no shortage of sights along the way

The Stourport Ring (83 miles, 118 locks, approx. 55 hours)
A busy week's cruising, some planning is required to get the best out of this ring as there's plenty to see and do along the way including the excellent Black Country Living Museum and the inland port at Stourport. The route takes in parts of the Staffs & Worcester and Worcester and Birmingham Canals, as well as part of the Birmingham Canal Navigations, including a passage through the heart of that city

The South Pennine Ring (71 miles, 197 locks, approx. 80 hours)
Not for the faint-hearted, this is the newest ring on the block made possible by the opening of the Standedge Tunnel. Both this landmark and certain locks on the Rochdale Canal needs to be booked so some forward planning is required. It is worth it as the route, which uses the Leeds & Liverpool and Rochdale Canals, is one of the most exciting on the system and has the distinction of crossing the Pennines twice, hence all the locks

The Thames Ring (245 miles, 175 locks, approx. 115 hours)
Travelling along most of the southern half of the Grand Union and emerging at the Thames at Brentford before heading upriver to Oxford and the entire length of the South Oxford Canal, this is an extensive route which includes a short stretch of tidal river. The South Oxford is many people's favourite canal, offering rural calm and pretty villages. This is, though, a solid two-week trip

The Warwickshire Ring (103 miles, between 94 and 107 locks, approx. 60 hours)
A challenging ring if attempted in a week, but the range of places to stop and visit means it can easily be stretched to two weeks. The ring takes in sections of the Coventry, North Oxford, Grand Union and Birmingham and Fazeley Canals, with an option at Kingswood Junction to divert onto the Stratford Canal. It is also possible to run into the heart of Coventry to visit the cathedral with other diversions available if taken at the more leisurely pace

Not Just Canals

There are over 3,000 miles of navigable waterways in England, Scotland and Wales, made up of a mixture of both canals and rivers, with each offering a diversity of experience. The rivers vary from the rural backwaters of the Fens to the grandeur of Old Father Thames, whilst the canals can also appear to be almost river-like at times but are more typically broken down into 'broad' and 'narrow' waterways.

It is not always easy to tell whether a canal is broad or narrow and the best way to be sure is by looking at the width of the locks (although some broad canals have two single locks). When the canals first began to be built it soon became obvious that some kind of standardisation was going to be needed if a true network was to develop. What emerged was the narrow 7ft (2.13m) -wide lock, typically 70ft (21.3m) long, although locks on some waterways, such as the Leeds & Liverpool Canal, are shorter (typically 60ft or 18.3m).

Favoured as they needed less water to fill, a key consideration in canal building, these locks were not without their disadvantages. Critically, they necessarily restricted the size of boats that could ply the canal, and incidentally gave birth to what we know now as the traditional narrowboat. At the same time adoption of this gauge also prevented more conventional river craft from utilising the canals, effectively sealing

Broad and narrow locks side by side on the Grand Union Canal.

Somerton Deep Lock on the tranquil South Oxford Canal, part of the Thames Ring.

'the system', and in time helped to contribute to their decline as it restricted the loads that could be carried.

The obvious alternative was, of course, the broad canal, defined as one with locks capable of taking two narrowboats side by side. The economic advantages of such canals was recognised when the new Grand Junction Canal between Braunston and Brentford was built in the broad gauge, and later in the 1920s when the remainder of the route into Birmingham was converted with the creation of the Grand Union.

Another clear distinction is between tidal and non-tidal waters. This is not a matter likely to concern those hiring a boat as holiday boats are rarely insured to use tidal waters and with good reason, as negotiating these waters is not for the faint-hearted! What's more, tidal waters require equipment such as an anchor, long ropes and a powerful engine that doesn't usually come as standard. For the experienced boater, however, studying the tide tables and making a dash for it can be an exhilarating experience, as well as providing the opportunity to construct more interesting routes.

Surprisingly, just under 10 per cent of the inland waterways are tidal and for the first timer the best bet is probably to test one's mettle on a short stretch, such as between Teddington Lock on the Thames and one of the entrances to the Grand Union.

A final distinction in the type of waterways is the 'Navigations', which usually pre-date the canals and describe rivers which have been cut, altered or sometimes diverted in order to make them navigable. Before the first wholly artificial canal was cut, there were over 600 miles of navigations in the UK, including rivers such as the Kennet, Aire & Calder, and the Weaver. Unlike canals, navigations remain part of the natural water system and as such are prey to the impact of flooding and therefore less reliable. In their favour, however, they tend to be wider and used by larger, sometimes ocean-going craft.

Who Is In Charge?

Responsibility for managing the vast majority of these waterways is divided between British Waterways (BW), which looks after the canals and a handful of river stretches, and the Environment Agency (EA), responsible for most of the major rivers. There are the odd exceptions to the 'big two' however, such as the Broads Authority which manages the Norfolk Broads, the Wey Navigations (part of the National Trust) and the Manchester Ship Canal Co.

Teddington Lock marks the beginning and end of tidal water on the Thames.

MAIN WATERWAYS BY TYPE

Main Broad Canals

Basingstoke Canal
Bridgewater Canal
Caledonian Canal
Grand Union Canal
Kennet & Avon Canal
Leeds & Liverpool Canal (60ft maximum length)
Monmouthshire & Brecon

Main Narrow Canals

Birmingham Canal Navigations
Birmingham & Worcester Canal
Coventry Canal
Llangollen Canal
Macclesfield Canal
Oxford Canal (North and South)
Shropshire Union Canal
Staffordshire & Worcester Canal
Stratford Canal
Trent & Mersey Canal (to Burton)

Main Tidal Waters

New Bedford River
River Avon (to Bristol)
River Ouse
River Thames (to Teddington)
River Trent (to Cromwell)

Non-Tidal Rivers

Lower and Upper Avon
River Great Ouse
Rivers Lee and Stort
River Nene
River Soar
River Thames (from Teddington)
River Trent (from Cromwell)
River Wey

Main Navigations

Aire & Calder Navigation
Calder & Hebble Navigation
Middle Level Navigations
River Witham Navigation
Sheffield & South Yorkshire Navigation
Upper & Lower Avon Navigation

Banbury Boat Festival.

SECTION B

Hawkesbury Junction, where the Coventry and Oxford Canals operate in parallel for a while, as if reluctant to meet.

Both BW and the EA make charges for using their waterways, with the former issuing a licence, the price of which depends upon the length of your boat, whilst the latter charges for registering and licensing craft.

Temporary registration is possible for those visiting EA waters, with three options of temporary licence available. It is also possible to purchase a Gold Licence, which gives access to the waters under the jurisdiction of both BW and the EA.

SECTION C

Boats, Buttys, Barges and Bargees

Two common misconceptions permeate conventional thinking about canal craft. The first is a confusion between narrowboats and barges, with the two terms often erroneously used interchangeably. The second is that the narrowboat/barge is the only type of craft that plies the canals, an assumption that does little justice to the rich variety on offer on the waterways.

Without further ado, let's get the first of these confusions out of the way. When considering the canals it is important to remember that they were not built according to some grand plan, James Brindley's 'Grand Cross' notwithstanding. When they were being built, the depth, width and size of locks on individual canals was understandably ruled by local conditions, and as such they varied.

The most significant difference was the width of the canals, and subsequently the size of the locks required. Early canals tended to be wider, most notably the Leeds & Liverpool, whilst the later canals, often referred to as the Midlands canals, were much narrower. This difference was reflected in the size of boats on these canals, with wider boats more efficient if the waterway could take them.

It is these usually cargo-carrying boats that are most correctly referred to as 'barges', their distinguishing characteristic being a beam much greater than the 7ft that limits the aptly named 'narrowboat', instead the size being determined by the width of the locks they had to use. In fact, barges tend to go up to 14ft wide in order to achieve maximum efficiency. Up to but not quite as, like the narrowboats (which are typically built to 6ft 10in), builders have discovered that it is wise to leave a little 'wriggle room' when it comes to locks.

Local circumstances also tended to influence the actual types of craft on individual canals, and canal aficionados know certain types of boats by nicknames, such as 'Joeys' or 'Barlow Boats', drawn from the boatyards that made them. Once again, the Leeds & Liverpool Canal is significant here as it has the distinction of being a broad canal but having locks that are typically only 60ft long, as against the 70ft that became the norm elsewhere. This led to a particular style of boat known, not surprisingly, as a 'short' – 14ft wide but only 60ft long.

The name says it all.

These short boats were carvel built wooden craft, with the planks that formed the hull being smooth and laid beside one another, a style that was in fact more associated with southern European styles of shipbuilding. Even within this style there were variations, with some having a round stern whilst others had a large square transom stern, i.e. using a crossbeam rather than one vertical sternpost.

These differences reflected the two 'cultures' the canal linked together, with the latter style in particular more common on the Yorkshire 'side' of

A Leeds & Liverpool 'short' moored at Skipton.

the Pennines. Getting agreement for this canal had been a feat almost as remarkable as the building of it, a fact that explains the canal's peculiar lock size which was designed to accommodate the Yorkshire 'keels' found on the rivers Aire, Calder and Humber, despite the fact that choosing this width made it impossible for a Mersey 'flat' to negotiate the waterway. On reflection, however, it is not too fanciful to see this as a deliberate ploy somewhere along the line.

Yorkshire keels and Mersey flats were each one of four general styles of barge, each linked to one of the four great rivers and estuaries of the time. These styles evolved over time to meet local needs, with each capable of working both coastal waters as well as rivers. Local skills and traditions then evolved once again to meet the challenges of the canals linking these rivers to the coast, and it is these historical roots that have helped contribute to the rich variety of craft that followed.

Keels were typical of both Yorkshire and the area around the River Humber and of the four main barge types these can probably trace their ancestry back the longest. With their round middles and bluff, almost flat fronts, these boats were not dissimilar from the longboats used to terrorise the east coast of England by the Vikings over a thousand years before. With their leeboards and single square sail added into the mix this comparison becomes even more stark.

Mersey flats described a style of boat that had become quite common before the coming of the canals along the rivers Dee and Weaver, as well as the Mersey and Irwell Navigation. These tended to have a round bilge and two masts which could be lowered or lifted out if required. The first mast would be about a quarter of the way down the boat with a mizzen mast on the stern deck behind the cargo. Unlike the keels, flats did not tend to have leeboards.

Early line drawings of the opening of the Barton Aqueduct, the defining moment of the first canal of the modern age, show boats looking like flats using the canal, although these were towed by horses rather than powered by the wind and only had one mast. That said, given the type of craft we associate with the canals today, it is significant that there is a mast at all and that this is carrying a rigged sail.

Further south, along the River Severn, barges tended to be modelled on the **trow**, a type of boat the plied both the inland rivers and the coastal waters around the south west. As such they tended to be robust craft, capable of withstanding both the notorious tides on the river and the choppy waters off the coast. They came in a range of styles, typically with open holds with extra canvas bulwarks laced up to a rail.

Upriver trows were mostly square rigged, with carvel style hulls again the norm, and a vertical transom stern where the boat's name and port would be displayed proudly.

Finally, barges in the south east tended to be modelled on the **Thames barge**, characterised by its flat bottom and large tan-coloured sails, along with masts and leeboards that could be lowered. These were typically crewed by two men or families and were highly manoeuvrable, capable of negotiating the crowded waters of the Thames, as well as the creeks and docks that fed into or off the river. Originally, 'swim-ended', that is shaped like a horizontal wedge, as time went on these became more streamlined.

Unlike the other three styles, examples of Thames barges are easily to come across today, both on the river and on the Grand Union Canal. Examples of keels, flats and trows are harder to come by, although some are preserved in the various waterways museums. The reason for this is simple – only Thames barges were able to justify themselves commercially until relatively recent times in the face of the demands from the canals. Severn trows, Mersey flats and indeed the Yorkshire keels all found they could

Early sail boats used to cross the Barton Aqueduct. (Manchester Central Library)

Sobriety at the Yorkshire Museum, Goole, is a good example of a Humber keel. (The Yorkshire Waterways Museum, Goole)

only go so far inland before their cargoes needed to be offloaded onto craft capable of passing through the narrow canals. As such their days were numbered and the narrowboat we know and love today began its period of ascendancy.

The actual origins of the narrowboat are unclear, but it is possible that the hand of James Brindley can be felt in their development. We have seen how boats with sails were the first to pass over his first great achievement, the Barton Aqueduct, but this was to be a temporary phenomenon. The canal he was building for the Duke of Bridgewater had one specific purpose – to transport coal from the duke's mines at Worsley to the growing metropolis of Manchester.

As it happened, the passageways into the duke's mines were extremely narrow. The coal would be mined, brought out into the daylight in containers and then transferred onto so-called 'box boats'. These were extremely simple in their construction, with straight oak sides and cross-planked elm bases, joined together by frames that were so pronounced that the boats became known as 'starvationers' as they looked like the ribs of a starving man.

Long and thin, it has been suggested that these became the template for later narrowboats. The Bridgewater Canal, however, had no locks, indeed it was in order to avoid locks that the Barton Aqueduct had been built. As such there was nothing to stop later canals from employing different styles. Once again, this is to underestimate Brindley's influence, for his was also the hand behind the second, and greater, canal of modern times, the Trent & Mersey.

If the Bridgewater had no locks, the Trent & Mersey had them in spades and, ever the pragmatist, Brindley would have seen the benefit of keeping to the sleek, no-nonsense style that had developed on his first great project. Slim, narrow locks would be much easier to build than large, barge-shaped ones. Furthermore, there was the little matter of a 2-mile tunnel just outside Stoke-on-Trent to build, the Harecastle, where once again the benefits of narrow over broad would have been self-evident. More by default than design perhaps, but the basic dimensions of the canal boat, its length, width and indeed height, had been decided, but not the exact style. So long as a boat could fit into this letterbox, there was room for some variation and boatyards across the country experimented with different styles, not least because they knew no better, and this was an age before 'Health and Safety' and uniformity ruled.

Boats continued to be made mainly of wood, although the maverick John 'Iron Mad' Wilkinson experimented with iron boats on the Severn in the early age of 'canal mania'. He was the exception, however; carpenters were easier to find than foundrymen, wood was easier to source and wooden hulls were easier to patch. The main differences in styles lay in how the hull was formed, with some taking a deeper and rounded shape and others adopting more of a V shape, and whether or not the boat incorporated a living space.

Boats without a living space were known as day boats, whilst cabin boats were built to travel the system, although every inch given over to accommodation was of course one less inch available for cargo, so the cabins tended to be almost ridiculously small. Day boats tended to be more common around the Birmingham Canal Navigations, whilst cabined boats ran the routes which linked Birmingham to the country's other main centres of population and industry.

These basic styles became more standardised with the coming of cargo carrying fleets, the most famous of which is probably Fellows, Morton and

SECTION C

Contrasting tillers on these two trad-style narrowboats.

A Fellows Sears and Morton boat beside a pair of trad-style narrowboats, recognisable from their characteristic bows.

Clayton. Started in 1837 by Thomas Fellows, the company really began to take off when his son Joshua took over and seized the opportunity created by the demise of the Grand Junction Canal Co. (GJCC) in 1876.

Joshua bought a number of boats from the GJCC and the company continued to grow when Frederick Morton joined in the same year bringing some investment capital with him, and the company was renamed to Fellows, Morton and Co. In 1887 the company took over the London and Midlands Carrying Co. absorbing the business of Thomas Clayton two years later, bringing about another name change to Fellows, Morton and Clayton (FMC).

The influence of the fleets is probably best illustrated by the 'Josher' hull, named after Joshua Fellows. This distinctive shape had a riveted wrought iron side and a 3-inch elm bottom. FMC spotted the potential of steam propulsion, the next great change in boat style, although the company can't claim to have pioneered this change. Its success lay in realising what it was they had acquired from the GJCC, who were among the first to utilise steam on the canals.

Using a coke boiler, these steam engine boats could carry less cargo – 18 tons against 25 tons that a horse-pulled boat could manage – but were considerably more powerful, which meant that they could pull one

Above: *Some boats can look more like houses.*

Left: *The beautiful highly varnished wooden boat* **Bronty** *seen entering Banbury Lock.*

or more unpowered boats, known as 'buttys'. These were like the old day boats, essentially a shell for carrying cargo. In their heyday, these would either be pulled behind the main boat or, if circumstances allowed, tied up alongside as a 'pair', which speeded things up when going through locks if the canal was broad.

Steam boats could also work 'fly', i.e. day and night, with the London to Braunston route a favourite, and the men who worked them gained their own place in the narrowboat hierarchy. By the nineteenth century this hierarchy had developed to the point where men working the narrowboats saw themselves as quite distinct, in their eyes superior, to those who operated barges.

Craft can come in all shapes and sizes.

The Thames may occasionally be mistaken for the Mississippi.

As such, it is not without some irony that narrowboat crewmen became known as 'bargees'. These were the men – and their families – who lived and worked on board their boats, their living quarters impossibly cramped and designed in such as way as to make use of every available inch. Some of the characteristics of this life are given in more detail in the chapter on 'Roses and Castles'.

Despite all the advantages offered by steam it never really displaced horses. That job fell to later diesel and semi-diesel engines, the first of which was introduced in 1912 (with semi-diesel engines heat had to be applied from the outside to get the engine to start). Diesel engines got over two problems the steamers never really conquered – the size and weight of the engine and the need to carry coal, both of which reduced the potential for cargo. Diesel-powered craft could carry 10 tons more than their steam-driven counterparts.

The coming of diesel occasioned another shift in basic design as room had to be made for the engine and efficiency demanded a shorter distance between the engine and the propeller, leading to the flattened back familiar on many boats today. This in turn led to the concertinaed Z-shaped tiller.

This style has become known as the '**trad**', or traditional stern, and is recognisable by its small unguarded deck. The big advantage of this

A Dutch barge cruising the Thames.

A pair of commercial boats tied together operating under one engine.

A delightful Thames skiff.

style is that in poor weather the helmsman stands forward of the rear doors and only the upper half of his body is exposed to the elements – the lower half being warmed by engine at the same time! In good weather helmsmen have also been known to steer when sitting on the roof.

Two other styles are still recognisable today. The first of these is the **cruiser**, which takes its name from river cruisers. These have large open decks at both the bow and stern which are often protected with a rail and usually incorporate some kind of seating. This is a fair weather style as there is very little protection for the helmsman in times of rain.

The final style is a compromise between these two and is known, perhaps inevitably, as semi-trad. Like the cruiser style, the hatch and rear doors are placed forward but the side walls continue from the sides to give more protected seating and a modicum of shelter for the helmsman.

As these descriptions would suggest, boat styles these days are driven more by personal preference than pragmatism, but through necessity have to remain within the constraints laid down over two hundred years ago. Modern ingenuity has continued to ensure that the limited space available is put to maximum effect and it is possible to find boats equipped with washing machines and even, in extreme cases, Jacuzzis, although the size of the water tank required to supply these luxuries is probably a question best left unasked.

Finally, it would be a mistake to think that only narrowboats wander through the waterways. It is true that they dominate the canals, but they share the water with more modern cruisers, which have many of the characteristics of their more traditional cousins, such as limited space and diesel engines, but almost without exception are made from glass fibre and are steered with a traditional wheel, and being much lighter are also easier to manoeuvre.

Mention has already been made of a hierarchy on the canals, and it is impossible to deny that for all their outward friendliness towards each other narrowboaters regard themselves as further up the food chain than their cruiser counterparts. Some have even been known to refer to them as 'plastic boats' and sneer at the profusion of outsized fenders the cruisers need to protect themselves, although such behaviour should not be seen as typical!

Finally, local ingenuity and individual preference mean that that there is no shortage of odd sights available on our inland waterways.

SECTION D

Roses and Castles

Oone of the most distinctive features of canal craft is their decoration. Bright, sometimes even gaudy, colours contrast with the usually dull coloured water, their reflections on the surface of that water doubling their impact. This tradition is as strong today as ever, perhaps more so given the much greater leisure time people now have to devote to their boats.

Go back a little, however, and this emphasis on colour seems less natural. The original canal boats were, after all, very much working craft, with those working them having little time and even less money to spend on fripperies. Boats, like the Model T Ford that followed, were black. It was not until some time into the canal age that the first references to what we regard today as traditional canal boat painting arose, with the earliest attribution generally accepted as one dating back to 1858 which described the style as being in 'the great teaboard school of art'.

This lovely put-down suggested that the style matched that seen on the cheap tin trays of the time. The date when it was written is equally significant, being nearly a hundred years after the Duke of Bridgewater opened the first commercial canal, suggesting that what we now regard as traditional canal boat decoration took a while to establish itself.

For the early part of the canal age, effectively the first decades of the nineteenth century, the canal companies owned most of the boats on the water and, given the heady activity of the times, had little time for indulgences. Any decoration there was tended to be added only when a boat was in the yard for maintenance or repairs – time which was kept to a minimum.

This therefore tended to be basic, with geometric designs a favourite, with diagonal lines criss-crossing each other and the resulting diamonds filled in with different colours, a style known as 'Scotch plaid'. The symbols of playing card suits were also popular, perhaps because these were widely recognised, with many on the waterways probably having 'learned their numbers' from playing cards, but more likely because of their associations with good luck.

Any other decoration tended to be confined to possessions or practicalities. Separate parts of the craft might also be differentiated by colour, with the hatches marked out in one colour, the decks in another and the bow and stern in yet another, just to distinguish them; with a universal black not the most useful colour against a murky canal, especially in winter. In time, bottle green became a more favoured base colour, with blues, reds and yellows also beginning to creep in. The tiller and rudder were also favoured spots, with the former often given the barber's treatment, a style which might be carried through into the poles.

Equally, the insides of the boats would typically be dark and it is understandable that some colour would be not only aesthetically pleasing but also useful to help find things. Decoration would be done at the boatman's expense, but on the plus side they tended to have very few possessions and as such might take more pride in what little they did have.

Roses decorating a milk churn at the Bygones Museum, Claydon, on the South Oxford Canal.

Over time it seems that if it didn't have a pulse it was painted, with vibrant colours a favourite, giving an illusion of riches that their owners could never otherwise enjoy. Headlamps, watering cans, feed boxes, stools, tables, even spoons all gained a veneer of paint. Pride of place often went to the Buckby Bucket, the water container that sat on top of every roof, which given its prominence would be given special treatment. Even if it had a pulse it wasn't necessarily safe, with horse's harnesses another favourite target.

As for the boats themselves, innovation was slow. As the community of boatmen developed, the companies found that experienced crews might be more readily tempted to brightly coloured craft and they began to see the benefits of extra decoration. This did not detract from the fact that a laid up boat was a boat not earning money, so it is no

Canal artist Jane Selkirk at work.

It is possible that this boat owner is not a dog lover.

surprising that the styles that emerged were simple and easily replicated whilst at the same time suggesting some degree of ornateness.

The classic designs were those that incorporated variants on the theme of roses and castles – but why? Certainly, these were easy to paint, with much of the task left to an apprentice with the skilled hand only adding the finishing touches, but it doesn't explain why these subjects became so synonymous with the canals.

The disappointing truth is that no one really knows why roses and castles gained the place they did. It is sometimes suggested that there are links to the Romany culture, which shares many themes with canal boatmen, but attractive though this theory is there is virtually no evidence to support it. Comparisons can also be made with similar folk art in places as far apart as Scandinavia and the Indian sub-continent.

The truth is probably more prosaic. It is likely that the painters who spotted this new market simply echoed the styles that had proved popular in the nascent consumer goods industries emerging in the mid-Victorian period. Consequently, the link to the 'teaboard style' is understandable, but other influences such as mass-produced furniture

The Players sailor was another popular subject.

can also be seen, as can that of the gothic revival around this time, reflected in a penchant for sunsets and romantic landscapes. Perhaps just as significant were links to the decorations used on agricultural carts.

What developed was in fact a highly efficient style of painting, with flower heads – usually roses, but sometimes others, such as daisies, dahlias and pansies – created with a base decorated by a few swift brush strokes, with a few more adding some leaves within moments. Similarly, the long slim towers of a castle could be created quickly, with clouds, sky and maybe the odd mountain all dashed off relatively swiftly by an

It is hard to believe that all the good names have been taken.

increasingly practised hand. Churches, lighthouses and generic towers, or even country houses, also proved popular, but none could out-do the castle as the structure of choice.

Towards the middle of the nineteenth century the railways began to exert their influence and the economics of the canals began to change. More and more boatmen began to live on board and, as time went on, their wives and families joined them. Perhaps inevitably, this added impetus to the desire to spruce things up a bit. Often compared with showmen and travelling folk, boating families were part of a tight-knit community and intermarriage was common. The chances of meeting someone you were related to, not once but a few times a day, were quite high, and as such pride in a 'well-kept home', for their boat was their home, was high. Finer detail began to creep in, including circular lace doilies on the inside of portholes, acting as a form of net curtain, along with highly polished brassware.

Slowly, a new breed of boatman began to emerge: the owner/carrier, who proudly carried the label of being 'Number One'. Now unburdened by rent, these boatmen broke free from the confines of the carrying company and, having reaped sufficient rewards from their hard life, were able to buy their own craft. One of the freedoms this gave them was to decorate their boat as they chose, and it was from this period that the colours, motifs and canalware we associate today with the canals really took off.

Another freedom gained was the right to call their boat what they liked. Although named, company boats gave just as much prominence to the company name and number, with the town of origin thrown in as a crude form of advertising. Number Ones would often proclaim themselves loudly as just that and at the same time names became more prominent.

This tradition has continued and these days noting boat names is one of the most pleasing, and at times amusing pleasures of being on the canals, with a simple word or phrase often speaking volumes about the boat's owners' interests or past. Puns are popular, as are names that give a clue to how the boat was bought in the first place, whether that be *P45*, *Kid's Inheritance* or the name of a departed grandmother who left a legacy. Names often prove a useful ice-breaker at a lock or mooring and add to the modern-day community of the canals.

Decorative traditions have also been maintained, and if anything, enhanced. There are a number of skilled artists still plying their trade on canal boats, and classes are available from these and the various museums for those who want to know more. Finally, no boat show is complete without at least one stand selling what is now known as 'canalia' decorated with roses and castles, and no boat, be they privately owned or part of a fleet, is complete without a reminder of the golden days of roses and castles.

SECTION E

Different Users

According to the latest British Waterways statistics, boaters sit in a significant minority when it comes to visits to the inland waterways. Like all statistics, require some unravelling. What exactly is meant by each 'visit' and do they carry equal weight? Is a morning walk with the dog along a towpath the equivalent to a three-week cruise?

Even taking these reservations into account, it is interesting to note that around 300 million visits are made to the inland waterways a year, with just over 2 per cent of these made by boaters and their passengers using powered craft. By far the largest proportion of visits is made up by those on a walk, ramble or run, who account for nearly 40 per cent of the total, with a further 30 per cent taken up by those walking their dog.

Others featuring in the statistics include those visiting the waterways using an unpowered craft (less than half a per cent of the total), anglers (1.6 per cent) and cyclists (8 per cent). The remainder of visits are taken up by those visiting attractions and those simply using the towpath as a means to get from point A to B. It seems reasonable, therefore, to consider these other users.

Walkers

Given the aforementioned breakdown, it seems logical to start with those who walk (ramble or run) along the towpath. The attractions for this group are perhaps obvious; the wildlife, the solitude and quiet, the near-impossibility of getting lost and, significantly perhaps, the distinct lack of gradient. Then there is the added benefit of the companionship offered by boaters and other users, and the possibility of pausing by a bridge or lock to watch the passing traffic go by.

This latter activity is known as 'gongoozling', although no one seems certain why. One theory is that it derives from the Lincolnshire dialect words 'gawn' and 'gooze', both of which mean to stare or just generally gape or gawp, suggesting some kind of Fenlands origin – perhaps early navvies left the Fens to help build the canals and introduced these words into the canal lexicon, but this is pure speculation.

The appeal of water to walkers is understandable and the towpaths provide the basis for a number of long-distance paths. It is usually possible to locate a bed and breakfast close to the water using guides, such as the Tempus Towpath series, which are also useful in pointing out landmarks, diversions and, of course, pubs. The following list sets out a suggestion for the top ten waterside walks in the UK, by no means all canals, recognising that one advantage walkers have over boaters is that they do not have to stick to navigable courses.

TOP TEN WATERSIDE WALKS IN THE UK

Angles Way – *A 77-mile route along the Norfolk/Suffolk border, following the Little Ouse and Waveney rivers from the Norfolk Broads to the Suffolk Brecks, starting at the mouth of the River Yare. From the coast at Great Yarmouth this route goes on to take in broads, lakes and marshland. Although easy going, good planning is required for places to stop*

The Bridgewater Canal – *40 miles of heritage as you pass along the waterway where it all began. From Leigh and the junction with the Leeds & Liverpool, to Preston Brook and the tunnel which marks the start of the Trent & Mersey, this walk takes you along the ochre-coloured water of Worsley and by the modern-day Barton Aqueduct. At times delightful, at others industrial, this is one for the historians*

The Caledonian Canal – *An unusual walk in that only 22 of its 60 miles are along towpaths, the remainder being by natural lochs, including the infamous Loch Ness, which makes it unique and earns it its place in this list. Cutting Scotland in two, despite appearances this is in fact a relatively straight-forward route, following a path known as the Great Glen Way. Start at Fort William to get the prevailing wind at your back*

The Grand Union Canal – *At 140 miles, the Grand Union is the granddaddy of canalside walks. Linking England's two largest cities, it begins and ends with distinctly urban landscapes, but in between lie surprisingly long rural stretches through the essence of shire England. Highlights include Stoke Bruerne and its museum and the Hatton Flight of locks outside Warwick*

The Kennet & Avon Canal – *Three waterways for the price of one, this walk takes in the two rivers in its title as well as the man-made section linking them. Linking Reading and Bristol, with Bath, Bradford on Avon, Newbury and numerous smaller towns and villages along its almost exactly 100-mile length, it is easy to do this walk in short stretches. The Caen Hill Flight at Devizes is a particular highlight and the Avoncliff Aqueduct provides a platform to admire the Avon*

Llangollen Canal – *Essential in any list of waterside walks, if for nothing else than its ability to deliver not one but two spectacular aqueducts, including the highly photogenic if hard to pronounce Pontcysyllte. Again, not overendowed with places to stop, this route might be more appropriate for those prepared to carry a tent. Its remoteness is part of its charm, though, with spectacular scenery and some interesting architecture along its 46 miles*

SECTION A   PART OF OUR HISTORY

Top: Worsley on the Bridgewater Canal, Britain's first inland 'port'.

Above: A boat carrying the Grand Union Canal Carrying Co. livery.

Opposite: The potters around Stoke were early advocates for the canals as they made it much easier to transport raw materials in and their delicate finished goods out.

The Rochdale Canal – *At only 33 miles, the shortest route in the list, this walk links the quintessential mill towns of Sowerby Bridge and Hebden Bridge with King Cotton itself, Manchester. Recent restoration makes this one of the newest routes on offer and combines industrial architecture with some spectacular Pennine scenery, with steep-sided hills coming right down to the water's edge*

The Severn Way – *One for more hardened walkers, the longest waterside route in the country covering 210 miles from its source at Plynlimon in deepest Wales to Bristol. The formal route combines countryside and waterside paths and its reputation as being not for the inexperienced is reinforced by the fact that it drops over 1,500ft along the way. Given its length, it comes as no surprise that there is a variety of landscapes, although the crystal clear water of the river remains a constant*

The South Oxford Canal – *Many people's favourite stretch of canal, although the towpath is not all it could be in parts and the price of the rural tranquillity it provides along its 49 miles is the need to cover reasonable distances between stopping points. Starting at the junction with the Grand Union, the walk passes through Cropredy, Banbury and Kidlington before releasing itself to the glory that is Oxford and the Thames*

The Thames Path – *Another source to sea route. Its 194 miles start in the deepest Cotswolds and gradually change in character as the river widens out after Oxford. A well-marked National Trail, although it was only designated as such ten years ago, the Thames has everything, from* Three Men in a Boat *innocence to hardened tourism at Henley and Windsor, and the familiar sights of the capital*

The Thames Path was formalised only relatively recently.

An angler on the Grand Union, watching and waiting.

Anglers

If it was not for the boats, there are times when anglers might legitimately feel as if the canals were made for them. It is often said that angling is the country's largest participation sport, and at times along the towpath it is easy to believe this, especially if there is a match on. Even when the anglers are absent they make their presence felt – they are the reason that you can see sequences of numbers along stretches of the towpath.

The fishing rights to large sections of our canals and rivers belong to angling clubs and associations, and whilst it is often possible to purchase day tickets it is best to know your ground before you start to unpack your kit. That the canals are so popular with anglers may in part be put down to their proximity to large centres of population, making it easy for those looking for a break from the hurly-burly of urban life. Weekends can be particularly busy and boaters need to be wary of where they moor on a Saturday night as it is possible that when drawing back their hatch on a Sunday morning they find themselves wedged between two earnest looking anglers.

It is fair to say that anglers and boaters don't always rub along. Skippers should try their best to do all they cannot to upset the angler's sport, but there are times when disturbance is unavoidable, causing the patient banksmen to reel their line in or raise their rod. That said, the very act of raising a rod to allow a boat to pass can sometimes seem to be timed to perfection, with the chosen height just enough to prevent the dangerous hook snagging anyone lying on the roof. Watch a boat pass through a competition on a narrow canal and it is like watching the swords at a guardsman's wedding rise in a wave over the boat.

Equally, to the fisherman boats can seem to take an age to pass (it is etiquette to slow down), and that is before the issue of wash is discussed. Boaters also need to recognise that their voices carry over water and as such it can be advisable to reserve any comments they may be

SECTION B   A NETWORK

Top: *Braunston, a pivotal point in 'the system'.*

Above left: *Great Haywood marks a junction on the Four Counties Ring.*

Above right: *Gargrave on the Leeds & Liverpool Canal represents the northernmost point of the main system.*

Opposite above: *Locks of the Thames can take as many as four narrowboats side by side.*

Opposite below: *Gailey Wharf on the Staffordshire & Worcester Canal is a feature of both the Birmingham and Four Counties Rings.*

thinking but do not necessarily wish to share for the pub or dining table later on in the day.

Unpowered Craft Users

Canoes and other unpowered craft are popular on the canals as they offer fewer hazards and possibly because the bank is never that far away should things go wrong. That said, the canals are not free from hazards and canoeists have to take notice of navigation signs and of other traffic on the water, although in reality whilst the maxim that 'steam gives way to sail' still holds, the stark truth is that it can be much easier to manoeuvre a canoe out of a potential clash than a narrowboat.

For the more experienced canoeist it is the very presence of potential hazards that contribute to the fun, and it is possible to see groups of canoeists riding rapids or slaloming through barriers, with weirs along rivers or points where a river meets canal favoured spots. A less welcome hazard is locks, where canoes need to be carried, with some offering 'portage' points which make it easier to get in and out.

Although it is possible to canoe down most inland waterways in the UK, the emphasis is on the 'most', with sections of the canals, such as tunnels, off-limits and access to rivers at the discretion of the relevant authority or, where relevant, the owner. Local waterways offices usually sell permits, whilst membership of the British Canoe Union includes the right to ply the canals and the River Thames.

Perhaps the best way to begin canoeing is through a club, of which there are plenty, and the best way to find a club is through the British Canal Union whose website (www.bcu.org.uk) also includes some useful background information on getting started.

Even 'gongoozlers' need to rest sometime.

Still waters.

SECTION C   BOATS, BUTTYS AND BARGEES

Top: **Scorpio** *and* **Malus,** *two boats ordered as part of the expansion of the GUCC fleet in 1935 and today restored Heritage Working Boats.*

Above: *A modern-day commercial narrowboat selling coal from the water.*

Opposite above: *The names of some of the old fleets remain alive through the efforts of restorers.*

Opposite below: *Narrowboats and river cruisers share the waterways without bother - usually!*

Cyclists need to get a permit from BW to ride the towpath.

The Devizes to Westminster Canoe Race

The longest non-stop canoe marathon in the world, the Devizes to Westminster runs over the Easter weekend and attracts hundreds of paddlers in a range of classes who compete over the 125-mile length of the course. The race began with a challenge to complete the course in under 100 hours, with the first to complete the course being the local scout group. These days the winners tend to get close to the 15-hour mark, paddling through the night, although more usually it is completed over the four days of the Easter weekend. The race starts with the Kennet & Avon Canal, proceeds on the Thames from Reading and finally enters the Tideway, or tidal part of the Thames, at Teddington. Critically, paddlers need to estimate how long it will take them to get to Teddington and time their start accordingly. If they get this wrong they may find that the tide is against them when they get there, which would have a seriously detrimental effect on their overall time

Other unpowered craft can range from rowing and sailing boats to windsurfers. Of these only rowing boats are really practical on the canals, and rowers break down into those who do so 'seriously', using light-weight craft that sit low in the water, and those whose intent is much more leisurely. Those in the former category can learn more through the Amateur Rowing Association (www.oara-rowing.org). Perhaps one of the sights of the summer by the rivers is of a party negotiating a channel in a river skiff, although whether any of these trips match Jerome K. Jerome's memorable (fictional) journey recorded in *Three Men in a Boat* is open to question.

Sailing is also popular, with beginners directed towards the Royal Yachting Association (www.rya.org.uk) who also provide courses in the correct handling of narrowboats and a weather eye over the sport of windsurfing.

Cyclists

Many of the attractions of the canals for walkers also hold true for cyclists. Unless otherwise stated, it is usually fair to assume that it is okay to use the towpaths for cycling (there are the occasional exceptions), although this is less true for river paths, where cyclists should check access beforehand.

British Waterways do expect cyclists to have a permit, however, and to display it on their bike, but this is easily done online via their www. waterscape.com site where there is also a downloadable list of available towpaths.

Canoeists meeting the reality of a lock.

SECTION D ROSES AND CASTLES

Top: *A classically simple geometric design on the back of a narrowboat.*

Above left: *Decorated Buckby Buckets are often given special attention due to their visibility.*

Above right: *Pots and pans are not immune from the paint treatment.*

Opposite above: *A particularly unusual wooden tiller with some castle thrown in for good measure.*

Opposite below: *Signwriters and artists remain in demand today.*

A travelling Punch and Judy show that entertains children from the side of a boat. (Courtesy of Allan Ford)

Few would argue with the assertion that when it comes to cycling, the Kennet & Avon is the canal equivalent to Milton Keynes, with well-made paths and plenty of places to hire and repair bikes along the way. Many cyclists have discovered that not only do canals offer excellent long-distance routes, but they can also provide very useful cut-throughs in built-up areas.

Care needs to be taken elsewhere, though, as not all towpaths are cycle friendly and an unexpected rut taken at speed can quite easily lead to an early and unwelcome bath. Brambles and other vegetation can also present a hazard at face, and importantly, eye height, and the use of a cycling helmet is recommended.

SECTION F

Getting Afloat

SECTION E   DIFFERENT USERS

Top: *Non-serious walkers are the most frequent users of the towpath.*

Above: *Cyclists, anglers and boaters all using the towpath.*

Opposite above: *Sailing boats tend to be more suited to rivers than canals.*

Opposite below, left: *Cyclists are well provided for on the Kennet & Avon; this hire stop is at Bradford on Avon.*

Opposite below, right: *An example of boaters and anglers existing in harmony.*

For those looking to experience the waterways on a boat there are two basic strategies to getting afloat: you either wade in gently and let the water take your weight, or you jump in and hope for the best. The former of these options is, of course, the more sensible but that does not stop an awful lot of people selecting the latter. Which you choose probably depends upon your temperament and how steep a learning curve you are prepared to tolerate.

Wading in gently involves research, patience and ideally a bit of real-time experience, either as a passenger on someone else's boat or as skipper of a hire craft for a week. Jumping in is much quicker and involves simply buying your own boat and learning as you go – after all, how complicated can it be? The answer is pretty complicated, actually, and although the essentials can be grasped fairly easily, the devil, as always with these things, lies in the detail.

Anyone with enough funds can get afloat. You do not need to pass a test, something which is sometimes all too apparent. Enjoying yourself once you get there requires a little more thought about what it is you are looking to achieve, what sorts of things you enjoy (and what frustrates you), your physical and mechanical abilities and what proportion of your life (and wallet) you are prepared to devote to this new activity.

This chapter sets out some of the issues you need to consider, raises some questions you might want to ask yourself and points you in the direction of where you can get more advice. Much of what is covered here applies to both the leisure boater and those looking to live on board their boat, although Chapter 8 covers the ins and outs of this in much more detail.

Hiring

The most common piece of advice offered to would-be boaters is, if you have not done so already, to test the water by hiring. Whilst this gives a useful taster, do not be fooled into thinking that it is exactly the same as ownership though. Hire boats tend to offer a careful blend of easy maintenance and high levels of kit and comfort, features that won't necessarily be replicated in your own boat. Hiring also avoids the inconvenience and worry associated with ownership, along with moorings and all the relevant paperwork.

Hiring undoubtedly has its advantages, however. You get to feel how to handle a boat and get a taste of the lifestyle and people attracted to boating. It can also give you a good insight into what makes a boat work for you – which features do you value and which are less important?

Are you happy building up your bed every night from what was the dining table in the galley (not always easy after a few drinks), or would you really value a permanent double bed? Do you want a television or computer access? What kind of bathroom and toilet arrangements are you most comfortable with? Just how good are you are learning to duck and keeping your (limited) space tidy and efficient? Which part of the system do you like the most? What size of boat suits you?

These are all questions worth knowing the answers to before you embark upon the process of buying, and the following list offers a selection of hire companies spread across the network to get you going:

SELECTED HIRE BOAT COMPANIES

Company	Contact	Waterway
Cheshire Cat Narrowboat Hire	01274 884094 www.cheshirecatnarrowboats.co.uk	Shropshire Union and Llangollen
Kate Boats	01926 492968 www.kateboats.co.uk	Grand Union
Lee Valley Boat Centre	01992 462085 www.leevalleyboats.co.uk	Rivers Lee and Stort
Middlewich Narrowboats	01606 832460 www.middlewichboats.co.uk	Trent & Mersey
Oxfordshire Narrowboats	01869 340348 www.oxfordshire-narrowboats.co.uk	South Oxford
Pennine Cruisers	01756 795478 www.penninecruisers.com	Leeds & Liverpool
Reading Marine	0118 971 3666 www.readingmarine.com	Kennet & Avon
Rose Narrowboats	01788 832449 www.rose-narrowboats.co.uk	North Oxford
Scotland Canal Holidays	01691 774558 www.scotland-canal-holidays.co.uk	Forth & Clyde
Shire Cruisers	01422 832712 www.shirecruisers.co.uk	Calder & Hebble

In addition, the following operate out of various locations:

Alvechurch Waterways Holidays	08708 35 25 25 www.alvechurch.com	Nationwide
Anglo-Welsh	0117 304 1122 www.anglowelsh.co.uk	Nationwide
Black Prince Holidays	01527 575115 www.black-prince.com	Nationwide
Blakes Boats	0870 2202 498 www.blakes.co.uk	Nationwide, including the Norfolk Broads

SECTION F   GETTING AFLOAT

Top: *A typical hire boat.*

Above: *A small river cruiser offers a relatively low-cost way to get onto the water.*

Opposite above: *Waterways festivals are colourful affairs and a good way to get acquainted with the boating sub-culture.*

Opposite below: *Marina moorings tend to be more organised and protected.*

Nothing quite beats the pleasure of having your own boat to yourself.

An alternative way to experience boating with the absolute minimum of fuss is to take a hotel boat holiday. As their name describes, these are floating hotels where you can get as involved as you wish on the physical side of a cruise and can expect a reasonable level of food and comfort. Hotel boats tend to hunt in pairs, with one offering rooms and the other dining facilities and back up. Boats are staffed with experienced crew who know what they're doing, but beware, this is not a cheap holiday. There is a good list of hotel boat companies at: www. canals.com/hotel_bt.htm.

TEN TOP BLOGS

If you want to get an insider's view of what it is like to own a boat you can do worse than consult some of the many blogs available on the net. At the time of writing the following were amongst the most active:

www.afloat.org.uk – London's canals on a Dutch Barge
www.nb-globetrotter.co.uk – Based on the Kennet & Avon
www.grannybuttons.com – Probably the grandmummy of them all
www.jannock.blogspot.com – Based on the Grand Union
www.ladyjogearman.blogspot.com – Follows the building of a narrowboat
www.moore2life.blogspot.com – Continuous cruiser
www.nbherbie.blogspot.com – Continuous cruiser
www.ramyshome.co.uk – Continuous cruiser
www.richardandmary.blogspot.com – Continuous cruiser
www.starcross.squarespace.com – Continuous cruiser

Buying

As this chapter has already hinted, forewarned is forearmed when buying a boat for the inland waterways. Before taking the plunge, it is a good idea to check that you have some answers to some basic questions:

- Who is it for? – Consider how many berths you are going to need. If there is just the two of you do you anticipate having guests? If it is to be a family boat remember that young children have an alarming tendency to grow into gangly adolescents.
- What is it for? – Assuming you are not intending to live on board think about how often you are likely to use the boat, and what proportion of visits will require an overnight stay. If you do not want to load and empty the boat each time you visit how much storage will you need? If you are looking for something to pootle about in on sunny days you may not need any sleeping accommodation at all.
- Where are you going to use it? – If you are going to confine yourself to the canals then a narrowboat would be usual, although a glass fibre cruiser can fit the locks and bridges just as well. If you

SECTION G   GETTING ABOUT

Top: *If possible, sharing a lock can share the work, as well as save water.*

Above left: *Be prepared to queue at locks during busy times.*

Above right: *The Dundas Aqueduct, one of many on the waterways system.*

Opposite above: *A lift bridge on the South Oxford Canal.*

Opposite below: *Turning is a delicate balance between speed and direction.*

want to enter coastal waters however you'll need something different. If you are not confined to narrow canals you may want to consider a barge of some kind.

Equipped with this insight you basically have three options when it comes to buying: buying new, buying second-hand or buying with someone else.

Buying New. Ironically, buying new can take the longest time of all and tends to be the preserve of those with a lot of money, often people who have recently retired and anticipate spending a large part of the year afloat, if not permanently. This is because most boats are built to order, although there are sometimes boats available from stock, notably smaller craft fitted out to preset layouts.

Having a boat built to order means, of course, that you have a great deal of control over what you get. The tradition of different boatyards having their own styles and approaches continues to this day, but within certain common standards. Almost universally, narrowboats come with steel (or occasionally aluminium) hulls, conform to one of the three styles described in Chapter 3 and range from around 30ft long to 70ft, with options at 44ft, 50ft or 55ft and 60ft. River cruisers tend to offer greater variety, although these are produced using standard moulds.

Boatbuilding is a highly skilled, capital intensive business, and whilst most builders are highly reputable it is not unknown for the companies to be better builders than businessmen. As such, those buying a boat should make sure they have a good contract (the British Marine

Some boats require muscle power to get going.

Federation offers a standard format – 01784 473377) and staged pay-
ments can be a good idea, as can a finish date. Buying direct from a
builder is more common with narrowboats than glass fibre cruisers,
which tend to be sold through dealers.

The Canal Boatbuilders Association (01952 813572) produces a book
called *How to Buy a Boat for Canal or River* but old canal hands will
have a good idea of the sort of layout they want. Otherwise it is worth
visiting one of the various boat shows where boatbuilders put their
boats on display, allowing you to walk around them and get some
advice. These can get booked up though and you may have to arrange
'slots' beforehand. The main boat shows are:

- The London Boat Show – London Docklands, January
- The National Boat, Caravan and Outdoor Show – Birmingham
  NEC, February
- Crick Boat Show (British Waterways) – Crick, near Rugby, Spring
  Bank Holiday
- National Waterways Festival (Inland Waterways Association)
  – Different location each year (canals and rivers), August Bank
  Holiday weekend

If you are useful with your hands and find you have time hanging on
them, you may wish to consider fitting out your boat using a shell provided by a boatyard. This can be a cheaper option, if you are happy not
pricing up your own time, but is not for the faint-hearted. Like all DIY,
fitting out on your own typically takes much longer than you thought
it would, although you will have the satisfaction of calling it your own
by the time you've finished.

Buying Second-hand. This is the quickest way to get afloat, but the
principle of *caveat emptor* (buyer beware) rules here. There are no log
books or service records when it comes to boats and the market is far
from perfect, which means agreeing a fair price is a matter of judge-
ment. An out of water survey is more than desirable, it is a necessity.
This does represent a risk, however, as the cost of the survey is the
responsibility of the potential purchaser and as such the investment
may be lost if the news is bad. Surveyors advertise in the canal press
and most boatyards will be able to recommend one.

One of the few pieces of paper that offers some information is the
four-yearly Boat Safety Certificate (see below). Torn between demands
for convenience and comprehensiveness, this has been altered considerably in recent years and, according to your point of view, has either
been watered down to the point where it has become a tick box exercise
or become more sensible and user-friendly.

Two things can be said about a Boat Safety check – it gives an insight
into things you cannot readily see (the electrics, ventilation, gas) and
if a boat has failed a check this is probably a warning. Do not assume,
however, that the Scheme covers everything. In recent years insurers

SECTION H   LIVING ON BOARD

Top: *A practical place to keep heating fuel for the liveaboard is on the roof.*

Above left: *Make sure the lifebelt and other safety equipment is to hand.*

Above right: *Mini gardens on the roof can often betray a liveaboard boat.*

Opposite above: *Good access to water becomes a necessity if your boat is also your home.*

Opposite below: *A fire, flowers and television aerial in place – looks like a liveaboard.*

have taken to demanding separate out of water surveys on older boats as they do not consider the Scheme to be an adequate assessment of relative risk.

When buying a boat second-hand, therefore, consider not only whether the size, layout and quality of fittings are what you are after, but whether the engine, systems and, most importantly, the hull have been maintained. As when buying a house or a car, look to see if your potential investment has been 'loved'. Has there been any investment in it? Are there any bad smells or signs of lack of basic maintenance? Is there any sign of rot or pitting? *The Inland Waterways Manual* (see 'Learn More and Links') gives an excellent list of things to look out for.

Above all, lift the engine hatch. A poorly maintained boat will show it in its engine hold – look for oil and diesel leaks, signs of equipment used for maintenance and what condition the batteries are in. If you can, get a mechanic to give it a 'once over' as there are few things worse than having an engine pack in on you miles from anywhere, or in a lock!

These points are raised to protect the unwary and are not meant to put you off. The boat market is surprisingly, well, buoyant, and there are plenty of excellent second-hand boats available. People upgrade or downsize according to circumstances and boating can be an activity carried out for a few years before individuals move on to something else, constantly releasing fresh boats onto the market. Well-maintained boats can even appreciate in value, although they should not be bought as an investment – your return is the pleasure you get out of it.

As with second-hand cars, when it comes to the actual process of buying the options are either to do the whole thing yourself or go via a third party – in this case, a marine broker. A good broker will act a bit like an estate agent, producing flyers, contacting interested parties, advertising and generally handling the whole sale – charging the seller a fee. They tend to operate out of marinas, which means it is possible to view a few boats in one go, although the better brokers have also embraced the internet. The best way to get an idea of what is on offer is to consult one of the main waterways magazines, which are packed with boats for sale every month. These are:

- *Waterways World* (01283 742970 – no website)
- *Canal Boat* (www.canalboatmag.co.uk)
- *Canals and Rivers* (www.canalsandrivers.co.uk)

These magazines also periodically publish surveys of boatbuilders, if you go for the buying from new option.

Before leaving the subject of second-hand boats it is worth raising the option of buying an ex-hire fleet vessel. Hire boat operators tend to 'churn' their craft fairly regularly, offering a ready supply of usually well-maintained, well-kitted out but perhaps not particularly imaginatively named or painted boats. All the points raised above still pertain, but these can provide a good 'entry-level' craft. It is true that they may not have been given the same love and attention an individually owned boat would enjoy, but narrowboats in particular can take a fair bit of abuse and come out smiling. You will also need to factor in the cost of a fresh paint job, which will run into thousands depending on size.

Buying With Someone Else. If you like the idea of owning a boat but cannot justify the cost, another sensible option is to spread the cost (and joys) of ownership with others. There are two ways of doing this: through a timeshare or syndicate.

Timeshares may be something more usually associated with foreign holiday apartments, and the principle is much the same. Basically, you buy a period of time on a boat for the same week or weeks each year. This tends to be more cost effective than simply hiring, but you do not tend to be guaranteed the same boat – on the other hand you do have the option of cruising different canals with the multi-site operators. Equally, as with property, timeshare buyers need to test claims that it is possible to swap or sell on weeks at a profit.

The main canal timeshare operators are:

- Canaltime - www.canaltime.com
- Ethos Narrowboats (Stratford Court Cruisers) - 01386 768 500 or www.cascadas.co.uk
- Shakespeare Classic Line - 01926 314958 or www.narrow-boats.uki. net

A more usual way of buying with someone else is to get involved in a syndicate. This is 'proper' ownership where syndicate members own a 'share' of a particular boat and equally share the costs of ownership with others, although crucially these are spread over a wider base.

Such arrangements can be put together independently or through a specialist company with the maximum recommended size of syndicate usually around a dozen. This size gives each member four weeks a year, although once the less comfortable parts of the year are removed this becomes between two to three weeks. Clearly, the fewer members the greater the time, but also the greater the cost.

Depending on how the syndicate is organised there needs to be some kind of mechanism for agreeing upon the scheduling of weeks, maintenance and money, but the internet has made all this much easier. Another important group decision is the progress of the boat, as whilst one advantage of syndication is picking the boat up at different points on the system, people's needs have to dovetailed.

It also helps if you know some of the people involved, although it is in the nature of syndicates that people move on and the sense of 'all friends together' that a syndicate may start out with tends to dissipate over time. On the other hand, syndication means you get to know the

SECTION 1   FLORA AND FAUNA

Top: *Cobwebs are a sure sign that summer is drawing to a close.*

Above: *Swans rarely refuse a proffered crust.*

Opposite top: *Hedgerow fruits ripe for foraging in the autumn.*

Opposite below, left: *Not all wildlife is as it seems.*

Opposite below, right: *Sloes hanging like grapes and just as ready for harvesting.*

Brokers tend to offer a wide selection of boats to view and inspect.

layout and quirks of a specific boat and means you can share some of the pride of ownership.

Keeping Afloat

Once you have yourself afloat, a reasonable consideration is how much it costs to stay there. Like most assets, a boat incurs certain annual fixed costs and in the case of a craft on the inland waterways these come under five headings.

The Licence. British Waterways charges for the privilege of using their waterways, for which you get access to the water and use of the facilities they provide, such as water points and rubbish and other waste disposal. It should be noted that this does not cover the whole inland system, with the Environment Agency responsible for the rivers Thames, Nene, Great Ouse and Medway; although it is possible to buy a Gold Licence which covers each others' waters. In addition, there is a smattering of smaller navigation agencies covering waterways such as the River Wey, Basingstoke Canal and the Warwickshire Avon, and a separate licence for the Scottish Waterways.

The cost of a licence varies according to the size and type of a boat but can vary from around £400 a year for a 30ft boat to nearer £700 for a 70ft one. The good news for canoeists is that they are covered if they are members of the British Canoe Union, otherwise canoes and unpowered craft must be licensed.

Insurance. In order to get a licence you must be able to demonstrate that you have third party insurance for at least £1 million. This sounds a lot but is not too onerous, with insurance for a second-hand, mid-sized boat at around the £100 a year mark, or less if you do not go for a fully comprehensive policy, although this is advisable and constitutes a marginal extra cost.

The third significant outlay is **Moorings.** If you have a canal passing the bottom of your garden then you are extremely lucky. For everyone else there is the issue of finding somewhere convenient and safe to leave your boat. One option is a designated long-term towpath mooring, for which you will need a permit from British Waterways with the cost depending on the location and the length of your boat. For this you tend to get a length of bank and little else, although depending on how lucky you are you may or may not get some convenient parking. Each region of British Waterways has a mooring officer, but the reality is that most of the best spots have been taken and as a newcomer you may initially be obliged to settle for what you are given and get on a waiting list for a better spot.

Another option is a marina, of which there are a growing number. These tend to cost two to three times as much as a towpath mooring, but you do get access to facilities such as electricity, showers, parking and maybe a clubhouse, as well as security. Mooring in marinas tends to be pontoon based. As with housing, mooring prices vary by region. A marina in the Midlands might cost between £1,500–2,000 per annum for a 60ft narrowboat, but further south these prices will easily double. One alternative can be to join a boating club, where you can get non-towpath side bankside moorings and some facilities.

Then there is **Maintenance.** As with cars and houses the secret here is to keep on top of maintenance and budget for a major outlay every second or third year – although the four-year cycle of the Boat Safety Scheme can act as a blunt reminder. This is effectively a boater's MOT and exists to make sure a boat is safe from the normal hazards of fire, explosions and pollution. As such ventilation, wiring, gas pipes and so on are all subject to a survey by a qualified surveyor, although the Scheme does not cover the hull.

Regular jobs include an annual engine service, hull blacking and fresh anodes to prevent rusting (every two to four years according to choice) and paintwork. Depending on how things go, the cost of these and general repairs is probably around the £500 a year mark, although this is a median figure.

Finally, there are **Running Costs.** These are not too bad, with diesel engines extremely efficient, requiring the leisure user to fill their (large) tank probably only once a year. At the time of writing this would cost anywhere between £50–80, although the issue of whether canal boats would lose their access to pink agricultural diesel was a hotly contested one. Gas is another cost, depending on usage, as are pump outs, typically between £10–15 per tank (some boats have two), with a family on board requiring a pump out per week. Water, typically, is free if you use the public taps. Marinas may charge.

SECTION J   INDUSTRIAL ARCHAEOLOGY

Top: *The recently restored Anderton Boat Lift is a fine example of both industrial archaeology and the energy of modern restorers. (British Waterways)*

Above left: *Most bridges have their own number, making it easier to place where you are.*

Above right: *The 'modern' Barton Aqueduct is an impressive swing bridge which moves with the water inside it.*

Opposite above: *A classic canalside wharf by the north portal of the Blisworth Tunnel.*

Opposite below: *The Caen Hill Flight outside Devizes on the Kennet & Avon.*

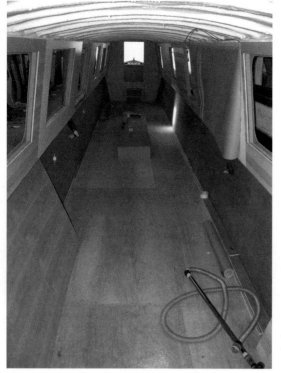

A new boat in the process of being fitted out. (Courtesy of Allan Ford)

Finally, if you own a narrowboat you should expect the unexpected, so be prepared for the occasional unbudgeted bill – in other words, do not commit yourself to your limit: have a contingency.

All this may seem as if the costs are steadily mounting, and to a large extent this is the case. Boating is not a cheap pastime but it is a rewarding one. Perhaps the best way to look at it is by comparing the cost of taking a family on holiday – owning and running a boat costs roughly the same as a one-week package holiday for four, but you do have access to it all year round.

SECTION G

Getting About

SECTION K   RENAISSANCE...?

Above: *The National Waterways Museum in Gloucester. (National Waterways Museum, Gloucester)*

Opposite above: *Once almost filled in, today Banbury's canal is the centrepiece of a modern shopping centre.*

Opposite below: *Today leisure is the name of the game for the canals.*

Like most simple things, managing a boat on the inland waterways can seem very complicated if you focus on all the component parts. In practice, familiarity and experience go a long way and most regular boat owners learn by encountering and then solving problems – so the next time they know what to do. For many, solving these problems is half the fun, although it may not always seem that way when you are dealing with them!

This chapter sets out some of the basics of getting about – some dos and don'ts; what to do when things do not go exactly to plan and some tips on safety. Like your boat, however, it can only skim the surface and readers are highly recommended to consult 'Learn More and Links' for more fulsome guides. If you intend becoming a regular boater it is also recommended that you consider the excellent one-day Inland Helmsman's Certificate, run by the Royal Yachting Association (see the waterways press for providers).

Safety Tip 1
Make sure the safety aids are in place, serviceable and to hand – fire extinguishers (make sure they are in date), fire blanket, the lifebelt and life jackets

Boat Basics

Before you even start to get going, it is a good idea to get to know your boat. The diagram on page 96 highlights some of the most basic elements of a typical narrowboat, and although these vary in practice on other craft, the fundamentals will remain the same, i.e. a means of propulsion and steering will be required, along with a lifebelt and other items of basic kit.

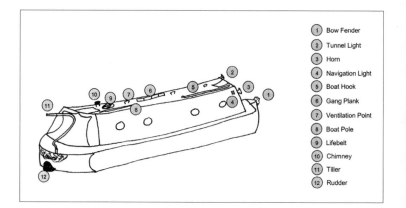

1. Bow Fender
2. Tunnel Light
3. Horn
4. Navigation Light
5. Boat Hook
6. Gang Plank
7. Ventilation Point
8. Boat Pole
9. Lifebelt
10. Chimney
11. Tiller
12. Rudder

The key parts of your boat.

Other essential items may sit inside the boat and before setting off it is worth just checking you have got the following on board:

- Mooring ropes
- BW key
- Torch
- First-aid kit
- Windlasses
- Hammer and mooring stakes
- Maps/cruising guide
- Gas
- Diesel
- Water

The most basic item you will need, however, is a skipper – and only one. The person in control of the boat should be just that. Decisions need to be taken all the time and it is better if there is one clear voice, not a committee, issuing them.

> **Safety Tip 2**
> *Never use your body or an arm or leg to lever a boat away from a mooring or obstacle. Your bones are not fenders and stand no chance against the combined force of a boat and the water*

Getting Going

Most boat controls are very simple. There is the throttle, upright for neutral, forward for forward and back for reverse, usually accompanied by a knob to put the engine into neutral when the throttle is upright, and a tiller or steering wheel for direction.

Steering wheels act as you would expect, turn right to go right and so on. Tillers are less straightforward. Here you need to push in the opposite direction to the one you want to go in, and this can take some getting used to. The faster the boat is going the more responsive it will be as more water is passing by the rudder. Good steering is about getting a balance between speed and manoeuvrability.

Boats tend to pivot at a point a third or a half from the bow (front), which can be disconcerting as it means one end of the boat is going one way and the other the opposite. The 'pivot point' is easier to spot if you are steering from the back, as is the case with most narrowboats. Cruisers also suffer from something know as the prop effect, where the propeller tends to push the boat to one side.

To get going, start in neutral with some revs, check the channel is clear and that in pulling out you are not about to push the stern and the propeller into some silt, and then release the (previously slackened) mooring ropes, making sure the crew is back on board before setting off.

SECTION K   RENAISSANCE... ?

Top: *Perfect solitude.*

Above: *Waiting your turn.*

Opposite above: *Canals for all.*

Opposite below: *Mass rallies returned to the canals in 2006, fifty years after they were first invoked, as a means of drawing attention to the plight of the waterways. Here, over fifty boats block the Mailbox TV Studios in Birmingham. (www.grannybuttons.com)*

Safety Tip 3
Be rope wise. Too many accidents happen because of shoddy ropes.
Always tidy them up and make sure they are in a state to be thrown
when necessary without catching someone or something

Keeping Going

Once you are underway it is best on most waterways to stick to the centre channel, where it is deeper, unless directed otherwise, for example by river buoys. You might think this is plain sailing but there are elements that conspire to confuse you.

These include the wind, which may push the boat about or suddenly build up when passing an open field (to counteract this you need to 'crab' or steer into the wind), and the bank effect. The latter happens when you pass close to a bank or another boat and manifests as a sucking of the boat towards the other object.

When you need to stop you need to use the reverse gear to slow the boat down. Boats, like cars, have momentum, and quite a lot of it. Unlike cars, they do not have brakes. On the subject of reversing, going backwards is an art form on most powered inland waterways craft for one simple reason – there is much less water for the rudder to deflect.

As such, tiller movements tend to have to be much more exaggerated to have an impact when reversing, and going backwards for any distance is not a recommended activity for the novice – if you miss a mooring spot then by the time you realised it you have probably lost it; another good reason for not going too fast.

Missing a destination may mean you need to turn your boat. This is simpler in a cruiser with its responsive steering and generally shorter length. Narrowboats, however, are advised to turn only at designated turning points. If you are on a wide enough stretch of water you can turn, but make sure the banks are not going to snare you first – you will need some leeway.

Turning points are also known as winding holes, as in the days before engines skippers would use nature to push the boat round. These days the procedure is to gently put the bow into the tip of the winding hole (never the stern, this may damage the propeller), making sure you touch the deepest part of the hole gently. Then apply revs in forward with the tiller pointing the way you want to go. The stern will move around until you are on the other side of the winding hole. Finally, swing the tiller the other way round and reverse off until you are clear and then apply forward gear.

Safety Tip 4
Never jump off a moving boat in a lock. The sides may not be as
firm as they appear and are often slippery. Current in a lock can
also cause the boat to move about erratically

Once you are on your way there are some basic ground (water?) rules, many of which are simple common sense, others more a case of accepted etiquette. Here is a list of ten 'dos and don'ts':

1. When passing a boat coming towards you the rule is 'port to port', i.e. keep to the right
2. Passing a boat going the same way as you, i.e. overtaking, is acceptable, but if possible make your intention known to the other craft beforehand. Make sure there are no bridges, bends or other craft coming, and putting a spurt on simply to grab the next lock is considered very bad form
3. Be water wise in locks. Wherever possible share locks with other craft and if you know someone is not that far behind have the courtesy to wait for them
4. When leaving a lock check to see if anyone is coming towards it. It may be possible for you to leave the gates open, saving you and them a job
5. Navigation channels on rivers are marked with buoys. Facing upstream red buoys are on the right and green on the left, the opposite going downstream
6. Remember, steam gives way to sail – craft with an engine should give way to canoes, rowing boats and the like (even though their boats are usually much less responsive!)
7. Do not use marinas for turning unless it is indicated that it is okay to do so
8. Slow down long before approaching moored craft, as it is not just when passing that you create disturbance in the water – pass as slow as practicable, causing no wash
9. Also slow down when passing anglers (it is simply polite) and when approaching bridges (it may save a lot of problems if someone is coming the other way)
10. Do not moor near a lock – you will regret it as the current caused by locking pushes you around. Equally, do not moor near a bridge

Managing Obstacles

There is no shortage of obstacles to make your journey more interesting. The most iconic of these is probably the lock, although this section also looks at tunnels and bridges.

Locks come in different shapes and sizes but the basic principles remain the same. Ultimately the aim is to change level and this requires entering a chamber and moving some water. The diagram overleaf sets out a basic lock format with the chamber protected by two sets of gates at either end. The boat enters the chamber, the gates are closed and water is either released into or relinquished from the chamber, after which the appropriate gate is opened to allow onward travel.

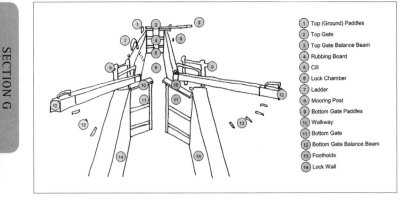

1. Top (Ground) Paddles
2. Top Gate
3. Top Gate Balance Beam
4. Rubbing Board
5. Cill
6. Lock Chamber
7. Ladder
8. Mooring Post
9. Bottom Gate Paddles
10. Walkway
11. Bottom Gate
12. Bottom Gate Balance Beam
13. Footholds
14. Lock Wall

The key parts of a lock.

Water is moved via paddles, usually operated by a winding mechanism from above with the paddles, or sluices, located in either the gates themselves or on the side of the chamber (known as ground paddles) – it should be obvious which need to be operated. Where there are both, the ground paddles should be opened first. On the canals gates are opened and shut using good old fashioned muscle power, although they are finely balanced and the beams used to move them are known as ... balance beams. On rivers these are often electronically operated.

Operating the winding mechanism requires a windlass or lock key, which fits over a spindle and provides leverage to operate a set of pinions or cogs. Performing this task is simple but fraught with potential danger. As such there are some windlass 'dos and don'ts':

• Make sure you are using the right size windlass, as locks do vary
• Wind slowly but firmly – there is a safety catch which will click as you turn. This will catch the mechanism if you let go so make sure it is working
• Keep fingers and clothes well away from the gearing
• Always wind a paddle down, do not just drop it – this can shatter a paddle and render it useless – and if you lose it get out the way as a windlass can easily fly off and hit you
• Make sure no one is standing between the balance beam and the water when opening a gate

It is not a good idea to simply open the appropriate paddle(s) to their full extent straight away: do it in stages, otherwise the boats may get thrown about by the forces that all the moving water unleashes. On this subject, the skipper needs to be on full alert when in a lock, this is not the time to make a cup of tea. If a lock is being emptied they need to keep way from the cill which the gate rests on at the back – it is all too easy to rest the propeller on this and tilt the boat, the most common cause of sinkings. It is also possible to get trapped on gates.

Also keep away from leaking gates and control the boat when water dynamics push it around – for this reason it is best to keep the engine on (although this is often not allowed on manned river locks).

Crew are best let off on approaching a lock to either help those currently working it or to prepare it. If they need to empty the lock the boat should stay well back. Once in the lock the boat can be steadied by passing ropes over any available bollards (especially advisable if it is a double lock being used by one boat), but not tied to them.

In double locks, single boats should start by opening the ground paddle on the same side as the boat, the water tends to bounce off the opposite wall and pin the boat usefully to the wall. Ideally, however, boats should share and if a steel narrowboat is sharing with a fibreglass cruiser the former should enter first and the latter exit first to minimise the risk of damage.

A further variety of lock is the staircase, where the bottom gates of one lock are the top gates of the next. These have rules of their own and tend to have lockkeepers on hand. If they do not look out for the board giving instructions before attempting the sequence. Similarly, guillotine and twin locks tend to be either self-evident or come with instructions.

Tunnels also have their own rules, also usually well displayed. The main issues are maintaining concentration when going through, being aware of other boats (some tunnels have traffic both ways), and the build up of fumes – for this reason no naked flames should be shown (including the stove). Headlights should be on before entering, a torch should be ready and it can be a good idea to put internal lights on too.

The crew needs to be mindful of the possible dangers and children should ideally be kept in the cabin. Travel should be slow (wash hitting a tunnel wall can throw the boat around), and if you manage to break down look out for the arrows inside which point to the quickest way out. If you are stranded blow your horn and make sure the engine is off. If *in extremis*, pole the boat out but do not swim to get help.

Bridges come in various shapes and sizes. The Leeds & Liverpool Canal is particularly noted for its swing bridges, the Oxford for its (usually open) lift bridges and the Kennet & Avon Canal for, well, just lots of bridges actually. Some require a BW key to operate them, others specialist keys such as a handcuff key and yet others a windlass. Most cruising guides will advise on what you will need. Treat bridges which require you to do some work as you would a lock, i.e. stop first, work out what is required and do not rush. Where you have to stop car traffic be courteous and choose your moment.

Static bridges also need to be treated with respect. The channel tends to narrow with the deepest part nearer the towpath side of the bridge, so aim to miss this by about 6–12in. Slow down, make sure no one is coming and ensure that any crew sitting on the roof come down.

Aqueducts are a particularly spectacular feature of most canals, although often more so for the spectator than the participant. The views from some, however, such as Pontcysylite on the Llangollen, can be the highlight of a voyage.

If necessary the electronic locks on rivers can be operated manually.

Safety Tip 5
*Avoid walking along the gunnel down the side of a boat if there is
a bridge coming up or if you are in or approaching a lock – and
remember the golden rule, 'One hand for the boat, one hand for you'*

Stopping

You can moor most places on the towpath (the general rule is you
can unless it says otherwise or it is plainly foolish to do so), and there
are a number of designated visitor moorings, often with restrictions, at
popular spots. If mooring away from these, it is a good idea to check
the soundness of the bank as you do not want the stakes to come free
during the night! Things tend to be more controlled on the rivers and
you may be charged a fee.

Approach a potential mooring slowly and have someone up front
checking out for depth and suitability. If it looks okay come alongside
gently, and if possible stop short of your intended spot so you can walk
the boat to where you want to be. Let some crew off with ropes and then
another member with the stakes and a hammer.

Stakes need to be driven in at an angle away from the boat and made
instantly identifiable, for example by putting an empty plastic bottle
over them. Try not to tie to trees and ensure that ropes do not stretch
over the towpath. Once the stakes are in get the hammer back on board
as it is all too easily forgotten.

Ropes should then be tied using a knot such as a round turn and two half
hitches. In some cases it may be necessary to use the gang plank to create a
safe route to shore, but this is unusual, and in crowded spots it may be necessary to 'double up' – with a boat's permission, which should be given.

On rivers, boats should moor with their bow facing upstream (into the
current), even if this means turning around to do so. Slack should also
be left in the ropes for a rise or fall in water level.

Troubleshooting

Of course, things will go wrong from time to time. Some of the most common problems are:

Electrical Failure. Once underway it can take a while to realise you have an electrical problem. Start by isolating its extent. This can help identify whether replacing a bulb or fuse will solve things. If it is general you probably have a battery problem. There are usually two batteries in the engine compartment and if you have no 'juice' it is probably because they are flat or the movement of the engine has shaken a connection loose. You may get away with topping up the distilled water, otherwise you need to get them charged. If you have returned to the boat and there is no power but you can hand start the engine, you can charge the batteries up again through simple cruising.

Fouled Propeller. This can usually be diagnosed by a terrible whining from the propeller or the boat travelling too slowly. The cause is usually weeds or some rubbish caught around the propeller or the shaft. The remedy is to moor up and undo the bolts from the weed hatch, sited underneath the tiller on the deck and usually marked. This provides direct access to the affected equipment, but naturally, the engine must be switched off first. After that it is a case of getting your hands dirty and a lot of fumbling around in the dark!

Gas Problems. If you smell gas, act quickly. If there is no obvious cause ventilate the area and get out. The most probable sources are either an oven tap or a faulty connection on the gas bottle, although this will, by law, be sited outside. The usual rules apply in this situation – no matches and do not fiddle with parts you do not understand. Gas kills and bottled gas is heavier than air, so it can sink and accumulate.

Getting Off Silt. It is usually impossible to gauge the depth of a canal and even the best skipper gets stuck on silt from time to time. When this happens you basically have three options.

The first is to get yourself off using the poles. This can work, but often does not. The poles tend to sink into the silt and there is the danger of stranding someone on the pole - funny to everyone except the victim. When doing this, consider where the boat is actually stuck and how weight on board is distributed – it is surprising what you can achieve by getting people to stand away from the stuck area!

The second is to rock the boat. This requires one or two people on each gunnel and literally rocking the boat off the silt with the free engine engaged at the same time. You will sense when you are floating.

The third is simply to wait and request a tow from the next passing boat – no one with any decency will refuse, but they will not thank you for joining you on the silt. So think about it first!

If stuck on silt, remember the golden rule that if you are going to use the engine to get off, you need the propeller in clear water. This can mean pushing the front of the boat even deeper into the silt in order to free the stern but this is a temporary expediency.

Man Overboard! Every skipper's nightmare, especially if a small child is involved. The first rule is, think before you act. Critically, someone absolutely *must* remain in control of the boat if it is not to add to your problems, which it can do in two ways – through its bulk and weight (the danger of crushing is one that should not be taken lightly) and through it is propeller.

As soon as the shout goes up the engine should therefore be put into neutral and the boat kept away from the person in the water – under no circumstances go into reverse, the person in the water may get sucked towards the propeller. The lifebelt or a rope should then be thrown out just in front of the person in the water. For this reason, the lifebelt should ideally be kept at the stern – if someone falls from the bow, the boat will pass them and if they fall from the stern then the distance is shorter. If the person is safe but cannot be brought on board (which can be tricky with an adult), and if they are away from the propeller, the skipper should head for the bank and effect a rescue.

If someone falls into a lock the procedure is different. For a start, the danger of crushing is multiplied by the presence of the lock wall and the difficulty of managing the boat. If the lock is in operation there is also the danger of water pushing or pulling them around. As such, the first thing to do is to gain control by putting the situation into 'neutral', shut down all paddles and get a line, or better still the belt, to the person overboard. Most canal locks have a ladder and this is probably the best way to get them out. If you try to pull them on board you may make the boat dangerously unstable. On manned river locks the lockkeeper will

Above left: *Winding gear is sometimes protected and may not need a windlass to operate it.*

Above right: *If you are lucky a lock keeper may help you out with the work.*

Left: *A lock-side paddle.*

Below: *Monkey Marsh Lock on the Kennet & Avon, a rare example of a turf-sided lock.*

Opposite below: *Bingley Five Rise is perhaps the best-known set of staircase locks on the system.*

Above: *Operating a swing bridge on the Kennet & Avon.*

Right: *Look out for special instructions, like here at Woolhampton on the Kennet & Avon with its tricky combination of river, swing bridge and lock.*

be trained in these situations. Anyone who falls in should take a good shower afterwards.

No water. Sputtering taps means you forgot to top up the water. With a family on board this needs to be done every other day, or whenever practical. It can be a good idea to have some bottled supplies on board for emergencies. If you know there is water but none is coming out the pipes it could be that the water pump is not working or a filter inside is clogged.

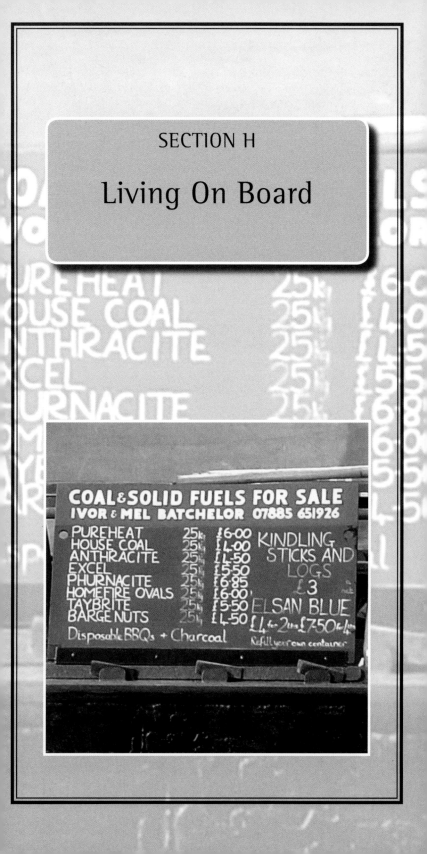

SECTION H

Living On Board

For some, simply visiting the waterways is not enough, they also want to live there. This is more than just a fantasy. Including coastal and inland waters, it has been estimated that up to 15,000 people live on board a boat in the UK. However, those contemplating joining them have to take a few things into consideration.

Taken on face value, the thought of living on a boat may seem a shift to an easier, less cluttered and complicated way of life, and in many ways this is true. It is a very different way of life, though, and one that involves compromises and a shift in mindset. Most important of all it means letting go of some things we generally take for granted and embracing fresh ways of living.

The first and probably most fundamental consideration is motivation – why do you want to become a 'liveaboard', as people who make boats their home tend to be known? Reasons depend on personal circumstances and can vary from the highly practical, such as finding a cheaper place to live, to a wish to embrace an 'alternative' lifestyle, and examples of both of these, and most shades in between, are easy to spot.

Liveaboards are not a distinct subculture though. They are a mixed group, each with their own motivations, needs and experiences. Talking to a cross section of them can be worth hours of research, and for those looking to join them tolerance and willingness to learn are useful starting points. Those who jump in and assume the role of 'instant expert' – a phenomenon the waterways are perhaps a little too prone to – tend to come unstuck.

Those motivated purely by cost are probably the least likely to last the distance. Successful liveaboards are those who achieve a happy balance of lifestyle and finance. Equally, having enjoyed a few holidays on a boat is not enough of a reason to up sticks. Hire boats are fitted out for a week, not in a lifetime – think about storage, laundry, heating and degrees of home comfort. Most of all, think bathroom arrangements. What you are prepared to put up with on holiday is unlikely to suffice if it is all you have got.

Liveaboards include those who tend to stay put on a permanent mooring, be that in a houseboat or a more conventional craft, and those who live a more nomadic lifestyle, known to the authorities as 'continuous cruisers'. In between, there are those with a mooring but who tend to go for long voyages, using their base as a wintering spot. A common feature of the waterways, these are typically people who have retired but retain a house or flat on land and enjoy a sense of being permanently on holiday and have an ever-changing view out their window. Indeed, the issue of land ownership can be a distinguishing feature amongst liveaboards. Those with permanent moorings may even own or rent a strip of land by their mooring which they then colonise with their 'overflow', such as somewhere to sit and eat, a fuel dump or general storage.

Next, it is worth moving on to consider some fundamentals. This is where the compromises start. Consider extremes. Whilst there are few things better than cruising along with a beer in your hand on a brilliantly

Hardy boaters have to be ready to cope with all conditions – even snow! (Courtesy of Allan Ford)

sunny day, think what it must be like when the temperature is minus ten degrees with the water frozen and your pump out toilet is full.

Consider also extremes of health. For those getting on in years or with young children, living on board may seem like an excellent adventure when you are full of the joys of spring, but being cooped up in a narrowboat bunk with a temperature, or worse, is not a lot of fun, especially if your GP (assuming you can register with one) does not make boat calls. Like it or not, some prejudice can take place in attitudes to boat dwellers amongst the authorities, which can mean that accessing healthcare might not be straightforward when a boat is seen as 'no fixed abode'.

Whether moored or not, liveaboards cut themselves loose from many of the ties that normally bind citizens to a wider society. These can be psychological, for example continuous cruisers by definition abandon a sense of being part of a fixed community, or just practical. Property dwellers enjoy the provision of a life support system that only becomes noticeable when it fails, such as the losing of heat, light, power, water and sewerage. On a boat, maintaining this system requires a conscious daily effort and advance planning. This can become second nature but liveaboards need to have the sort of mind that is happy to juggle these priorities.

This attitude can also be reflected in the view taken towards residential boats by local councils, not least in regard to Council Tax, with the regulations open to a variety of interpretations. Similarly, as you might expect, boaters have a right to vote – they are the true floating voters – but to exercise it they need to register somewhere. On a similar theme, having a postal address is another feature of modern life usually taken for granted by property dwellers but less straightforward for liveaboards.

All these considerations need to be taken into account. The good news is they are all solvable but, as this chapter has already highlighted, they may require compromises or a fresh outlook. Additional good news comes in the fact that some of the answers have been documented. Particularly useful is the publication called *Living Afloat* available from the Residential Boat Owners Association (RBOA) (see 'Learn More and Links').

Assuming these considerations can all be accommodated, there is a final tier of nitty-gritty issues that have to be taken into account. The most important of these is acquiring the right kind of boat. Some advice on boat buying is given in the 'Getting Afloat' chapter, but as has already been highlighted the demands placed on a residential boat will be different from those of a fun boat and will depend upon how your craft is going to be used. For example, if continuous cruising is your aim you will place a higher premium on the capacity of your fuel tank.

Equally, permanent boat dwellers will want to take into consideration the capacity of water tanks and the waste system. Heating can also be important (few holiday boats have much in the way of robust heating systems), along with the required fuel (wood stacked on the roof of a boat can often be a sure sign of a liveaboard), as will sleeping arrangements and storage. Access to basic life support systems and their ease of maintenance are another important thing to keep in mind, with the same true of the engine.

The design of storage space should also be considered and is an area where advice and experience can be particularly useful. The old bargees knew a thing or two about using space efficiently, but then they did not have cappuccino makers to find a home for. Nevertheless, it can be interesting to look at a few old boats to see what they used to do or to see what other liveaboards do. Lessons can also be learned from the caravan industry.

Moorings have also been mentioned. There are some designated residential moorings along the towpath, but the better ones with good access tend to be highly sought after. As with fun boat mooring an alternative is

When your boat is also your home, it is not always easy to stay tidy. (Courtesy of Allan Ford)

to moor at a marina, which although expensive can offer a sense of community. Non-towpath moorings are also available, often at boatyards or with cruising clubs, but these come with a landlord and the RBOA also produce a document called *Getting Residential Moorings Right.*

British Waterways has lists of residential moorings (www.waterscape. com) and the waterways press also publish occasional surveys. If you are really lucky you may have a stretch of water at the bottom of your garden, but this does not mean it is free. You need to get an 'end of garden' permit, typically charged at half the rate of equivalent nearby moorings, and British Waterways reserves the right to refuse them, for example if they are too close to a bridge or lock.

Last but not least, there is the issue of paperwork. Liveaboards need to licence and insure their boats, as well as comply with the Boat Safety Scheme, as set out in the chapter on 'Getting Afloat' – with one proviso. Those looking to become continuous cruisers on the canals can be exempt from the requirement to prove a permanent mooring. This does come with strings, however, and is an area which British Waterways, quite understandably, has tightened up on considerably in recent years.

Being a continuous cruiser means you are obliged not to stay in the same spot for more than fourteen days, and hopping back and forth between two spots does not count – you must show you are engaged on a 'genuine progressive journey'. Equally, the same spot does not mean the same mooring, but the same neighbourhood, i.e. if you are in one neighbourhood you need to be in a different one fifteen days later, although 'neighbourhood' is open to interpretation according to local circumstances. The onus throughout is on the owner to satisfy British Waterways' regulations.

Coldly looked at, the various considerations set out here may appear enough to put off all but the most determined. It is worth reiterating, however, that practically every problem has a solution and that all of the issues outlined here have been raised before, and there are places you can go for advice.

A wood-burning stove can be a cosy option for those cold winter nights. (Courtesy of Allan Ford)

For those with the right mix of motivation, character and sense of adventure living aboard a boat can be a real joy, but do not forget that it is a large step to take and one that needs to be taken with due consideration. Hopefully the points raised in this chapter will help guide those contemplating taking it.

Owning a boat is a bit like owning your first second-hand car – be prepared to spend time and money on keeping it going. Overleaf is a list of the top ten areas to look out for:

SECTION H

BASIC MAINTENANCE

The Hull – *Absolutely basic! Without a hull you have no boat. Below the waterline the steel is protected by 'black', usually bitumen, but this needs regular replacing, the frequency depending on how much cruising you do. As a rule of thumb, blacking on the four-year BSS cycle is generally a good idea. You also need sacrificial anodes which slow down the rusting process*

The Superstructure – *This is the bit you see and is attacked from above by the elements, so it is also prone to rust. Being within reach this can be tackled, but if left the one thing it will not do is go away. A good paint job helps, so do not skimp, especially on priming. Patches can be repaired but after a while it becomes all too obvious*

The Engine – *Most engines are pretty reliable but do not take yours for granted and make sure it is serviced annually, with filters and an oil change. If you know engines, give it a regular once-over and tweak as necessary; if you do not, leave well alone*

The Electrics – *Electrical systems vary enormously depending on the specification of a boat, although most run off 12V car batteries. There are usually at least two of these, and connections and distilled water need to be checked. Inverters and cut-ins, such as solar and wind generators, are useful but can complicate matters*

The Plumbing – *Most systems are self-contained and run on the same lines as a house, other than toilet waste. Pumps and filters are the most common problem areas, but care also needs to be taken to avoid freezing in the winter when systems have to be either drained or anti-freeze added*

Gas – *With gas bottles having to be kept outside, the main issues are ventilation and corrosion. Pipework and boilers should be left to CORGI registered experts*

The Galley – *Look out for accumulated debris around cooker rings; cobwebs and dust can build up remarkably quickly. Make sure the fire blanket is serviceable and keep an eye on the fridge, especially the seals and ice box if you have one*

Woodwork – *Ventilation is the key, as otherwise your wood will rot. Prevent condensation on the inside and maintain a good varnish on the outside*

Safety Equipment – *Maintenance of self and crew should really come first. Make sure the lifebelt and jackets are accessible and appropriate. Keep the fire extinguishers up to date and keep a useful first-aid kit – this usually means supplementing commercial kits with a few remedies*

Tools – *Do not get stuck! Adjustable spanners (large and small), screwdrivers, wirecutters, a hacksaw, a 'Stanley' knife and a hammer are all basics, as are some key spare parts (fuses, sealant, hoses, jubilee clips)*

SECTION 1

Flora and Fauna

One of the most satisfying pleasures of the inland waterways is the opportunity to appreciate nature. Beyond the occasional bird feeder or garden pond, few of us really have occasion to enjoy the diversity of wildlife that surrounds us. Wandering around the waterways offers the triple advantages of a constantly changing landscape, an enormous variety of species to spot, and most importantly the time and means to spot them.

Forewarned is forearmed, however, and it is useful to know what to look out for. British Waterways conducts annual wildlife surveys and these typically record around sixty different species ranging from the ubiquitous mallard through to the more exotic terrapins and Chinese mitten crabs. Some of these are native, whilst others are more recent introductions viewed with differing levels of welcome. Mink, for example, have become very common, and a menace, in a short space of time, whilst crayfish have taken over some parts of our waters, although those in the know have devised ways to harvest them!

This chapter provides a brief summary of the main forms of wildlife that can be spotted alongside our canals and rivers under five classifications: flora, fish, mammals and amphibians, insects and birds.

THE TOP TEN WATERWAY WILDLIFE SIGHTINGS	
Mallard	*Kingfisher*
Swan	*Water Vole*
Moorhen	*Bat*
Heron	*Grass Snake*
Coot	
Dragonfly	Source: British Waterways

Water Quality

First, a brief word on water quality. Compared to rivers, canals can seem murky and polluted, due largely to their lack of current and depth. It is actually possible for an adult to stand in the canals, although it is not particularly advisable, but in the centre of most canals mud tends to linger, and regular dredging, certainly along the towpath side, is a constant issue.

Murky yes, but polluted, less so. Although you would not want to drink it, canal water is in fact relatively uncontaminated by industrial pollutants. There are stringent controls on water allowed to enter the system, with most canals fed by their own managed reservoirs and, unlike some continental systems, it is strictly forbidden to discharge sewage from any source.

Problems tend to come from individuals, with litter a common issue around built-up areas (the cliché of shopping trolleys lining the bankside is often a justified one), and films of oil or diesel on the surface

After a while it is possible to become blasé over sighting of the glorious heron, but they should never be taken for granted.

SECTION 1

of the water are also not as rare as they should be, with one person's clumsiness or selfishness taking a long time to disperse.

Perhaps the best test of water quality is the diversity of flora and fauna it attracts, and if this is the case then it cannot be that bad! Not all the wildlife, however, is welcome, and rats in particular, although usually unseen, leave their own legacy. This is Leptospirosis, a bacterial infection carried in the rat's urine particularly prominent in slow moving, freshwater canals (salt tends to destroy the bacteria), which enters the bloodstream through cuts and abrasions.

The bacteria causes particularly nasty flu-like symptoms with fever, headaches and back pain, with an incubation period of up to twelve days, making it difficult to diagnose. In severe cases the victim can also experience jaundice, when the condition becomes known as Weil's Disease. Although cases are rare, these are serious illnesses and it is for this reason that **swimming in canals is not a good idea**, and those who do have to enter the water must make sure they protect any potential entry points.

Flora

Perhaps more by default than design, Britain's waterways provide a time capsule of the nation's flora. To some extent protected from chemical intrusion and saved from the effects of enclosure, it is possible to see wild flowers and funghi long since lost in more cultivated areas flourishing by the water's edge.

Swimming is strictly inadvisable in canals, crocodiles or not.

Towpaths act as a series of linear nature reserves, passing through a variety of different habitats from moorlands to meadows, with the canals themselves gouged out from most of the country's representative soils – from peat, through chalk, clay and gravel and even granite. What is more, these precious paths provide a breeding ground and channel for roots and seeds with the result that flowers lost to the country can sometimes appear serendipitously in the heart of our cities.

Even where the effort of cutting the canals had the effect of distorting the natural landscape, time has wrought its miracle and made it nigh on impossible to spot where man's labours end and those of Mother Nature begin. After two hundred years, embankments and cuttings have become the landscape and the natural order has reasserted itself.

The yellows of flag iris and marsh marigolds or kingcups mingle with the red of rosebay willow herb, whilst a variety of reeds and rushes appear, including the familiar reedmace with its spiked brown flower. By way of contrast the more delicate pendulous sedge, or the white flowers of ramsons and bear's garlic can also be seen. And in the case of the latter's cousin, the wild garlic, can be smelt.

Meanwhile, on the water itself, water lilies can often multiply to colonise the surface, the broad flat leaves slinking underwater on the approach of a boat as if pulled down by an unseen monster. Fennel leafed and curled pondweed are also common, as is duckweed which can spread rapidly to form a carpet from bank to bank. Other plants lurk beneath the surface and these we probably prefer to call weeds as they can be the boater's unseen enemy by fouling the rudder.

Between the towpath and the water lies the bank with its own distinctive foliage, including large rhubarb-like leaves which can act as a deterrent to mooring. Many banksides are only mown once or twice a year allowing wild flowers to flourish; wild primroses and even orchids being on display at different times of the year.

Of course, not all is beautiful and unusual and the towpaths also have more than their fair share of stinging nettles and brambles, so care should be taken when walking and, especially, when cycling. On the upside, however, in the right season it is possible to pause and gather hedgerow fruits including blackberries, apples and crab apples.

Fish

A canal without fish is unthinkable and, as the armies of anglers who line the towpath testify, fish are not something the canals tend to be short of. The accompanying list sets out the most popular species to be found in the canals, whilst some of our rivers are also known for trout and even salmon.

THE MOST POPULAR FISH SPECIES FOUND IN UK CANALS

Perch – *A greenish hue with black vertical stripes and an orange tinge on the edge of their fins and tails. Grows up to 6–8lb*
Roach – *Silver in colour with a lateral line on each side of its body, at home in weedy waters. Grows up to 2lb*
Carp – *Lots of different varieties, but the common carp has small uniform scales with a fat body. Usually golden/silver in colour, can grow up to 60lb and in the past was bred for food*
Chub – *Black/silver with a green back and silver sides and white belly. Carp have yellow/red fins and tend to be easy to catch. Can grow up to 4lb, but is rare at this size*
Pike – *A distinctive elongated body with a greenish/yellow topside and white belly. Each pike has its own markings, usually spotted in nature. Can grow as long as 4ft with recorded instances of pike as heavy as 50lb. A voracious carnivore and cannibal*
Bream – *Deep-bodied fish with compressed sides, the common bream found in the UK has a dark back often with a greenish hue and golden sides. The bream has a distinctive mouth, can live for up to twenty-five years and grow up to 12–15lb*

Mammals and Amphibians

It is not only humans who are attracted to solitude of the waterways. Equally, like most humans, the wide range of mammals who visit our canals and rivers are drawn by the idea of a quiet drink. If you are lucky you may spot a fox or badger taking a sip, but a more likely encounter

While some 'gongoozle', others turn their attention to the wildlife.

will be with a cow or horse, both of which are likely to regard you with an air of invaded privacy as you pass by.

When wandering along the canal you may hear a distinctive 'plop' as something falls into the water. This could well be a water vole, which swims under the water, unlike a rat which keeps its snout above the surface. The two are often confused ('Ratty' in *Tales from the River Bank* was in fact a water vole), with voles sometimes called water rats. Voles colonise banksides and their presence is a sign of clean unpolluted water. Their numbers had declined rapidly, not least due to the attention of the mink, but they are now actively encouraged and are a protected species.

Also in or near the water are toads and frogs, with the toad much shorter and shorter limbed than the frog with a dull brown or olive-coloured warty skin. Toads tend to emerge at night to feed and can seem quite clumbersome in their movements. Frogs on the other hand tend to be green, brown or yellow with a smooth skin. Both species often sit patiently by the side of the water where they could spot a grass snake. These are grey in colour and harmless; indeed they are likely to slither off or play dead when approached.

Also visible around dusk are bats whose swooping against a sky filled with a setting sun can be a spectacular sight. The most common variety by the canals and rivers is the tiny pipistrelle, which is rarely more than 2in long, although their wingspan can stretch to up to a foot.

Insects

Insects are, of course, the most plentiful source of species in the natural world, with over 20,000 different types in the UK alone. Not all of these are welcome and they may be viewed as both a blessing and a curse by the towpath visitor. They lie at the bottom of the food chain and as such are vital to the maintenance of the wildlife system. Luckily, the combination of the water and plentiful hedgerows, as well as numerous other places to lay their eggs, means that the waterways are a natural insect habitat.

Perhaps the most distinctive insect along the waterways is the dragonfly, with its brightly coloured elongated body and two pairs of wings. Although a common sight on the canals, dragonflies in fact spend almost all of their life underwater where they exist as larvae. Once hatched they are lucky to live for more than a few weeks, assuming they get past the first few hours of adult life when they are extremely vulnerable to predators while waiting for their wings to harden.

As if seeking revenge for this trial, dragonflies are voracious predators, with a large set of jaws and massive eyes. Dragonflies will eat other insects, taking them on the wing, and even tadpoles and small fish up to stickleback size. They are harmless to humans, however, and can even settle on a proffered finger. Dragonflies should not be confused with their smaller counterpart, damselflies, which tend to linger in vegetation and have a much lower profile.

The list of other insects alongside the canals is almost endless, from butterflies to surface dwelling insects, such as waterboatmen and pond skaters. As such, if this is an area of interest it is worth taking an identifier with you when patrolling the towpath.

Birds

Likewise, our canals and rivers are a haven for birdlife and barely a minute goes by without spotting some kind of duck, most probably a mallard but possibly a dark black moorhen, charcoal grey coot or, if out on a river, a grebe, with swans also favouring these waterways, although not exclusively. Grebes are particularly eye-catching with their habit of dipping under the surface and re-appearing a long distance away.

Also eye-catching are kingfishers. A sudden flash of blue can arrest the attention and cause you to search around for its cause. Highly defensive and extremely fast, you will do well to see a kingfisher, but it is worth the effort. Cobalt-blue in colour, these birds have bright orange bellies and a white bib. They feed off fish and appreciate slow-moving waters, hence their attraction to the canals.

A key feature of the canals is, of course, the heron. The first time you see one of these grey and gangly birds they look spectacular, not least due to their size – it is the UK's largest common bird after the mute swan. They also have a habit of remaining extremely still until you get close when they open their wings and flap awkwardly into the sky, normally describing a semi-circle before returning to their starting point. After a while, however, the towpath visitor can become blasé about these magnificent creatures, counting how many they manage to spot a day.

WILDLIFE BY SEASON

Winter

Winter is a time for rest when most wildlife chooses to recharge its batteries. Ice on the water can hide activity below as larvae get ready for the spring and the fish sit out the cold. Grass snakes are biding their time in old rabbit warrens. Birdlife is still visible, with ducks and herons hiding in sheltered spots and even kingfishers can be seen. It is also a time when other wildlife not so easily spotted in the summer might be seen, such as otters

Spring

Things kick into action with the warming of days. Toads, frogs and newts wake up and seek out the water to spawn, whilst grass snakes also make the pilgrimage to feed upon their efforts. Golden carpets of celandine line the banks, joined by the stiff leaves of the yellow iris, and as spring takes hold butterflies and other insects, such as ladybirds and bees begin to appear, followed by dragonflies. The hedgerows also begin to bud, whilst occasional bulbs familiar from the garden, such as crocuses, snowdrops and daffodils, appear in the least expected places. Spring is truly settled once the buds on the hedges turn into blossom and the first lambs appear, with the occasional hare bouncing around between them. Finally, the bird population is boosted by the return of migrants, such as swallows and swifts, and signs of nest building become apparent

Summer

Early summer sees the first fluffy chicks, which demand to be counted. Another sure sign of warmer days ahead is the appearance of the orchid-like orange balsam, as well as butterflies and dragonflies beginning to appear in the air. Wasps and bees also make their – not always welcome – appearance, although more agreeable perhaps is the distinctive sound of crickets enlivening the late summer evenings. Worth looking out for are the signs of activity from badger cubs, which are weaned from their mothers towards the end of May, with freshly dug holes as a tell-tale sign. All the birdlife associated with the waterways now comes into view, with chicks growing into adolescence and then adults, a sign that summer is progressing

Autumn

Hedgerow fruits ripen, begging to be picked as summer gives way to autumn and trees lose their leaves, depositing a kaleidoscopic carpet on the surface of the water. Migrant birds, such as warblers, feed off the plentiful insects and seeds, and ready to depart once again. The early mornings are marked by dewy cobwebs, which as time passes may even be captured in frost, making for exceptional photographs. Features of the summer disappear one by one and the countryside shuts down for another year

SECTION J

Industrial Archaeology

On first glance, the phrase 'industrial archaeology' sounds like a contradiction. Isn't archaeology about digging for Roman coins whilst 'industrial' is altogether more modern? In the end it all comes down to perspective. Just because it was more recent does not mean that the industrial age was any less important in informing and helping to shape the way we think and live today. Being more recent has the added advantage that plenty of examples are still around, meaning we have to rely less on reconstruction and computer aided graphics to get an understanding of them.

As we have seen, the canals were an essential part of the industrial age and some would argue that the waterways system is the best example of industrial archaeology – there have even been moves to make them a World Heritage Site. What better means, therefore, to appreciate the very best of Britain's industrial past?

British Waterways statistics report 2,739 listed buildings and forty-two scheduled monuments alongside the canals, and whilst not all of these are industrial sites the vast majority date from what we might call the industrial age. Many are easily passed without really appreciating what they are or the contribution they have made. Others may simply be seen as 'normal' structures still in use today and therefore not really monuments. The point is, history is all around when you cruise the waterways system. The trick is knowing how to spot it.

For our purposes, canalside industrial archaeology has been divided into three categories – buildings that served or serviced the canal, structures built to carry or bypass the canal, and a broader group called 'pointers'. To get the ball rolling the accompanying list provides a subjective assessment of the top ten waterside wonders, each of which is mentioned as this chapter progresses.

SECTION J

THE TEN WATERSIDE WONDERS

Attraction	Canal
Anderton Boat Lift	Trent & Mersey
Barton Aqueduct	Bridgewater
Bingley Five Rise	Leeds & Liverpool
Caen Hill Flight	Kennet & Avon
Crofton Pumping Station	Kennet & Avon
Falkirk Wheel	Union/Forth & Clyde
Foxton Inclined Plane	Grand Union
Harecastle Tunnel	Trent & Mersey
Pontcysyllte Aqueduct	Llangollen
Standedge Tunnel	Huddersfield Narrow

Buildings

Buildings that served or serviced the canal come in a number of guises. The most obvious of these are probably the various wharfs that still line

Tooley's Boatyard in Banbury, historic but with a modern veneer.

the towpath. In the heyday of canals every centre of population would have had at least one place where boats could stop and load or unload. Whilst many of these have now disappeared, others still survive, either as working boatyards, British Waterways depots or simply on their own.

Simple but effective, wharfs typically consisted of one or two buildings, an open area for storage and some good mooring. Others were more complex, such as Gailey Wharf on the Staffordshire & Worcester Canal with its elegant roundhouse, built to give a good view of approaching traffic. The wharf at Ayhno on the South Oxford Canal is perhaps more typical, with its brick-lined mooring, simple building and an awning for protection.

Workshops and docks tended to spring up beside wharfs, but because the activities taking place in these buildings have changed little over the past 200, it can be difficult to appreciate that still functioning dry docks and yards are in fact living examples of pre-Victorian industry.

Perhaps ironically, one of the most revered yards on the system, Tooley's in Banbury, also on the South Oxford Canal, is the opposite of this. Famous as the starting point of L.T.C. Rolt's classic book *Narrow Boat*, Tooley's yard was rescued from demolition and is today encased in a glass box, giving it a distinctively modern appearance.

Warehouses are another sight often associated with canals, and sadly many of these are in decline and very few are still in use. Often monolithic and with their backs turned to the canal, their very size seems to

A section of the lining used to restore the Blisworth Tunnel.

defy demolition, although some have been rescued through the expedient of being converted into homes. Long stretches of the Leeds & Liverpool Canal, through Stoke on the Trent & Mersey and outside of Birmingham at the northern point of the Grand Union all offer evidence of an age now gone.

Other more picturesque structures have attracted the attention of restorers, their original purpose preserved and presented to the public in the form of a tourist attraction. A good example of these is the pumping house, a necessary part of most canal systems through the need to pump water released by locks back up to the canal's summit.

Crofton Pumping Station on the Kennet & Avon Canal presents an excellent example, with its towering chimney imposing its presence

Shrewley Tunnel, with its own side tunnel for horses.

over the landscape for miles around. Inside it is possible to appreciate the scale of the task these old engines performed and how the energy was created to allow them to do it.

Elsewhere, once you get your eye in, it is possible to identify waterways offices and other edifices lining the bank. One of the easiest of these to take for granted is the canalside pub, often by a lock (allowing the boatman to slake his thirst whilst waiting for a lock). These are legion but often just look like pubs until you put your history glasses on and view them as vital supply posts on the canal network.

Structures

When the canals came they represented an imposition on the landscape and structures had to be built to allow the passage of the 'flat water'. Sometimes this meant carrying the canal over an obstacle, but sometimes it meant carrying the obstacle over the water. On other occasions the only answer was to go through the obstacle, either by using locks or, in more extreme cases, by digging a tunnel.

Tunnels are perhaps both the most impressive of all examples of industrial archaeology and at the same time the most modest. Viewed from the outside, a portal can be a disappointing affair, much anticipated but with little to actually see when you get there. Once inside though it becomes a little easier to appreciate the sheer effort and organisation that would have been required to dig the tunnel, especially when you consider that in the early years all the builders had at their disposal was sheer brawn, picks and barrows.

Each tunnel has its own history. Building them was rarely a straight-forward affair and some of today's survivors represent a second or third attempt. Many have also been the subject of recent restoration, such as Blisworth Tunnel on the Grand Union, where it is possible to see one of the concrete sections used to reinforce the tunnel by the western portal. The best example of this is also the greatest of the tunnels, that of Standedge on the Huddersfield Narrow Canal. Restored in 2001, this tunnel is over 3 miles long and is the longest, highest and deepest tunnel on the system. Finally, mention must be made again of the Harecastle, which although not the longest was the first major tunnel to be built on the system.

THE TEN LONGEST NAVIGABLE CANAL TUNNELS

Tunnel	Canal	Yards
Standedge	Huddersfield Narrow	5,698
Dudley	Dudley No.1	3,154
Blisworth	Grand Union	3,057
Netherton	Dudley No.1	3,027
Harecastle	Trent & Mersey	2,926
Wasthills	Worcester & Birmingham	2,726
Braunston	Grand Union	2,048
Foulridge	Leeds & Liverpool	1,640
Crick	Grand Union	1,528
Preston Brook	Trent & Mersey	1,239

SECTION J

Understandably, tunnels were only built where there was no alternative, i.e. where locks were not a practical solution. Locks came with their own complications, not least the need to feed them with water and their capacity to slow down traffic – although tunnels also usually represented a bottleneck, especially if their width only allowed for one-way traffic.

The one area where locks do score over tunnels, however, is their sheer grandeur. There is something about the sight of a long flight of locks clinging to a hillside that demands attention. Excellent examples of flights offering a vista include the Caen Hill Flight outside Devizes on the Kennet & Avon Canal, the Lapworth Flight on the Stratford Canal and the Bingley Five Rise staircase on the Leeds & Liverpool Canal.

Not all lock flights are so obviously picturesque, perhaps because of their location or because they are less concentrated, but this does not detract from their significance. One of the most notorious flights is 'Heartbreak Hill' on the Trent & Mersey which comprises thirty-one locks over a number of miles, or the Wigan Flight of twenty-one locks which carries the Leeds & Liverpool Canal up to the Bridgewater across a decidedly industrial landscape where, in its heyday, the light given out by the nearby blast furnaces of the Wigan Coal and Iron Co. meant it was never dark.

The completion of the iron Wolverton Aqueduct outside modern-day Milton Keynes saw the final completion of the Grand Junction Canal.

An air shaft from the Braunston Tunnel, easily missed amongst the fields that cover the top of the tunnel.

SECTION J

The Warwick Aqueduct on the Grand Union carrying the canal over the river below.

Often equally impressive to the eye are the aqueducts sometimes used to carry waterways over a valley or inconvenient gap. Once again, aqueducts represented a considerable challenge to the early canal builders and they were only used when locks were not a viable option.

Despite this, the first modern canal, the Bridgewater, astounded its doomsayers by including an aqueduct which was built over the River Irwell to avoid not only two flights of locks (at the time an equally untried technology), but also to prevent the Navigation Co. that controlled the river from charging extortionate fees to boats wishing to cross their waterway.

This aqueduct, the Barton just outside Lymm, remains an impressive example of the art, although the version on display today is not the original. No less impressive, the modern structure is a giant swing bridge which moves a whole section of canal to one side when required.

Indisputably the most impressive of all the aqueducts is the Pontcysyllte on the Llangollen Canal, begun by Thomas Telford in 1795. This has nineteen cast-iron arches, each with a 45ft span with mortar used in its construction, including a dash of oxen blood for added strength! Other shorter aqueducts are scattered over the system, and if travelling by boat it is easy to miss them altogether, their grandeur being better appreciated from a distance. Good examples of these include the stone Dundas and Avoncliff Aqueducts, close together on

Signs of the past are everywhere, you just have to look out for them.

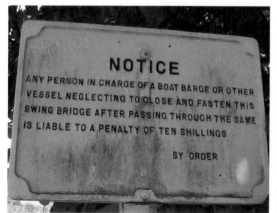

There is usually no shortage of instructions or threats around obstacles found on the canals.

This more contemporary milepost in Birmingham is also a kilometre post.

The north portal to Telford's successor to Brindley's Harecastle Tunnel.

the Kennet & Avon Canal, and the iron Wolverton Aqueduct on the Grand Union.

Not surprisingly, bridges are the most common structures seen on the canals and they come in all shapes and sizes. The classic stone-arched 'Brindley Bridge' has been incorporated into British Waterways' logo, and variations on this theme abound. Perhaps one of the most surprising 'finds' with bridges in archaeological terms is the number which seem to have no apparent purpose, providing clues to ancient footpaths or cattle runs. Equally, other aspects of a bridge, what it is made of, its type and size, all provide evidence of the surrounding economic geography when the bridge was built.

More details on the different types of canal bridges are given in the chapter on 'Getting About', but one or two features stand out. The first is what is known as a 'turnover bridge' where the towpath switches sides, as the bridge forms an 'S' shape to allow the horse pulling the boat to cross sides without needing to remove the towrope. Similarly, it is possible to spot gaps in some bridges to allow a towrope to pass through and where a bridge sits on a slight bend, the grooves cut by the ropes can be seen in the side of the brickwork or in the iron guard put there for the purpose.

Before leaving a discussion about structures, it is necessary to mention some of the more ingenious methods used to move whole boats from one place to another. One of these, the Foxton Inclined Plane on the Grand Union Leicester Line, transported boats on rails set into the side of a hill. Another, the Anderton Boat Lift on the Trent & Mersey, carried boats in cassions or chambers between the canal and the River Weaver below. Whilst the former is the subject of a restoration effort, the latter recently reopened after many years of dedicated fundraising.

Finally, although not strictly in the category of archaeology, the Falkirk Wheel, linking the Union and Forth & Clyde canals in Scotland, proves that the pioneers had no monopoly on inventiveness! Opened in 2002 this futuristic rotating boat lift allows boats to negotiate the 75ft between the two canals without the need for locks, the whole operation conducted using less electricity than a domestic shower.

Pointers

A final set of archaeological clues can be found in the signs, notices and markers that line the towpath. These can vary from mile markers, most notably on the Trent & Mersey and Grand Union canals, to a variety of metal notices giving instructions to boaters and wagons using the bridges over the canals, usually backed up by some threat of a fine if disobeyed!

Most bridges also carry markers, numbering the bridges off from the canal's start point. These make it easy to place where you are and can also provide archaeological clues, for example when the numbering loses its sequence. This is especially noticeable along the North Oxford Canal where a programme of 'straightenings' led to a number of mean-

Crofton Pumping Station on the Kennet and Avon and its imposing chimney.

Gloucester Docks, used by inland and coastal craft alike.

ders in the canal being cut off, along with any bridges on them. Not only did this have the effect of creating a confusing sequence but also led to a number of stranded 'orphan' bridges.

When it comes to industrial archaeology if you are prepared to look beyond the obvious and ask the purpose of canalside features, your enjoyment of the landscape will undoubtedly be much enhanced.

SECTION K

Renaissance... ?

After the war the waterways entered what looked like a final period of decline. This steady deterioration offered a marked contrast to the manner in which they had come about. Inasmuch as the foresight and sheer energy of the early industrialists had created the bulk of the system in a couple of decades, its decline was a much more drawn out affair. The commercial advantages offered by the railways, and then the roads, meant that left alone the canals could only offer a rearguard action against the inevitable.

Owners cut costs to the bone whilst boaters worked in conditions we would regard today as intolerable in order to keep traffic on the water. As it happened, external forces contrived to prop up the ailing system. Both world wars placed such demands on the country's transport infra-structure that (even) the canals were found a role, and in between these two seismic events the waterways offered opportunities for centrally financed job creation schemes during the Great Depression.

When the Second World War was finally over reality could be postponed no longer. In 1947 the railways were nationalised and the waterways, almost as an afterthought, followed suit. As the country picked itself up off its knees the neglected waterways found them-selves far down the pecking order for funds. By the 1950s the mood became more optimistic but the appetite was for things new, stylish and modern, for tower blocks and motorways, not reviving the past and waterways. With many of them now silted up and unnavigable, canals came to symbolise the past. Dirty, dangerous and decrepit, they became the target for campaigns to fill them in, to erase them from the collective memory.

This view was not universal. The year prior to nationalisation, a few canal advocates, including the writers Robert Aickman and L.T.C. (Tom) Rolt, came together to form the Inland Waterways Association. Bravely, these mavericks negotiated what remained of the waterways and waited for their time to come. Their efforts stopped the waterways from being entirely neglected and meant that there was at least a body to channel opinion when the tide of opinion began to turn.

It was clear that the canals could never again be a commercial proposition for trade, but the increasing affluence of the 1960s meant that there was another option. The birth of the 'consumer society' and increased leisure time meant that the waterways could be born again as a source of pleasure. Rather than being a national liability, the country's rivers and canals began to be seen as an asset.

It was a close run thing, and today's waterways user has much reason to thank the lonely voices in the wilderness who spoke up for the canals in the 1950s. More than simple fanatics, they lobbied the powers that be and proved highly adept at congregating to form rallies on threatened canals to raise public awareness and make the case for conservation.

Nowhere was this more so than at Banbury on the South Oxford Canal. Threatened with being filled in to make way for a bus station,

Trip boats help make the canals accessible for all.

thereby effectively decapitating the canal which provided a link between the main part of the system and the Thames, Banbury was the site of a major rally in 1955 involving 300 boats and 10,000 people. Their efforts were enough to provide a stay of execution and buy the time to allow the shift in emphasis away from cargo to leisure to happen.

In 1957 the Government established the Bowes Committee to review the future of the country's system of inland waterways. The Committee's report, published the following year, was ambivalent, but this was better than negative. It listed 800 miles of canal with an uncertain future and suggested that each canal be examined on its merits by a redevelopment committee.

It was enough. The canals were spared a Beeching-like rationalisation and as the 1960s dawned the idea that the canals could be cruised for pleasure was beginning to take hold. By 1963 the British Waterways Board was established and many canals were eventually re-classified as 'Cruising Waterways' in recognition of their new purpose.

A number of individual canal societies were formed, for both already navigable canals and those requiring restoration. From simply maintaining what they had, these bodies looked to improve them and even something that would have been unimaginable a decade before, to bring waterways back from the dead.

Progress was slow, as in many cases restoration meant the application of hard labour from volunteers giving their spare time, as well as a constant fight against both bureaucracy and mother nature. An early triumph was the Stratford Canal from Lapworth south to Stratford, which was reopened in 1964 after its cause was picked up by the National Trust. Others followed, albeit slowly, including the Ashton and Peak Forest Canals in 1974.

This showed that canals could be revived and ambitions grew. Perhaps the most spectacular success was the restoration of the Kennet & Avon Canal (opened in 1990 by the Queen) and the transformation of the canals in the heart of Birmingham around Gas Street Basin.

Birmingham's vision, seeing canals as something to be admired not hidden away, was soon replicated in other large cities, notably those in the old industrial heartlands which, coincidentally, also happened to

The canals have become part of the fabric of the nation.

be magnets for redevelopment funds. Manchester also re-discovered its canals and then, in an ironic twist, in the 1990s Banbury decided to redevelop its centre around a canal.

The next lucky break came with the establishment of the National Lottery. Good organisation and the ability to appeal to both heritage and the future, and to gather local government and other official body endorsement, all combined to mean that canal advocates were well placed to exploit both this new source of finance, as well as funds flowing from bodies such as Regional Development Agencies and the European Union (EU).

In 2000 the Government published *Waterways for Tomorrow*, a policy document which recognised the new reality and spoke glowingly of the importance of the waterways as a national resource. It was also interpreted as giving a green light for British Waterways (BW) to act more commercially, and they embarked upon a programme of waterside development and marina investment in a drive to establish financial self-sufficiency.

For some these moves were seen as controversial, taking the organisation's eye off the more critical tasks of dredging and basic maintenance. However, this criticism needs to be measured against a long-standing history amongst some of animosity towards BW, seen as the scapegoat for all the waterway's ills, right or wrong.

That said, during its recent history BW has embarked upon grand schemes, with mixed success, such as its plan for a fibre-optic pathway beneath the towpath and a national water grid. Perhaps it is simply the lot of quasi-monopolistic bodies to be the natural focus for grievances? Even in times of relative largesse there will always be differing views on the relative calls on resources between boats and boaters!

Either side of the Millennium, over £190 million worth of lottery funding was secured for waterways projects, resulting in the reopening of 200 miles of waterway. Notable successes included the re-opening in

2001 of the Huddersfield Narrow Canal, which included the Standedge Tunnel, and then in 2002 the Rochdale Canal. A statistic often quoted during this period was that more miles of canal were being re-opened per year than were built during the heyday of 'canal mania'.

These were golden days with some comparisons to the heady atmosphere of the canal mania years. It seemed that any project associated with the canals stood a reasonable chance of securing funding. This included not only the waterways but other expressions of the heritage they represented, such as museums. The number of waterways museums increased during this time, whilst those that were already established found it easier to attract funds.

TOP TEN WATERWAYS MUSEUMS

- Black Country Living Museum (0121 557 9643) www.bclm.co.uk
- Boat Museum, Ellesmere Port (0151 355 5017) www.boatmuseum. org.uk
- Canal Museum, Stoke Bruerne (01604 862229) www.thewaterway-strust.org.uk/museums/stoke.shtml
- Foxton Canal Museum (0116 2792 657) www.fipt.org.uk
- Kennet & Avon Canal Museum (01380 729 489) www.katrust.org
- London Canal Museum, London (020 7713 0836) www.canalmuseum. org.uk
- Merseyside Maritime Museum (0151 207 0001) www.liverpoolmuse-ums.org.uk/maritime
- National Waterways Museum, Gloucester (01452 318200) www.nwm. org.uk
- River and Rowing Museum, Henley (01491 415600) www.rrm.co.uk
- Yorkshire Waterways Museum, Goole (01405 768730) www.water-waysmuseum.org.uk

Meanwhile, in 2004 BW decided to exert a little more control over restoration efforts and announced a list of priority projects. To the disappointment of its supporters, this list did not include the proposed Bedford & Milton Keynes Waterway, remarkable for being a brand new waterway rather than a restoration, a step too far perhaps?

As recently as 2005, BW was confident enough to set a vision in its four-year plan to 'develop a network that would be used by twice as many people in 2012 as had used it ten years previously'. The maintenance backlog, which previously had the same reputation as a hospital waiting list in that it was taken as a given, the only question being its length, had, miraculously, been almost eliminated.

The future looked bright when suddenly the waterways were forced to wake up and stop dreaming. In August 2006 budget problems within DEFRA, the government department responsible for providing much of BW's funding, led to sudden and largely unexpected cuts in grants, which also led to job losses and a real threat, not only to planned

The Canal Museum on Devizes Wharf. (Devizes Canal Museum)

The Stratford Canal south from Lapworth was an early success by the restorers.

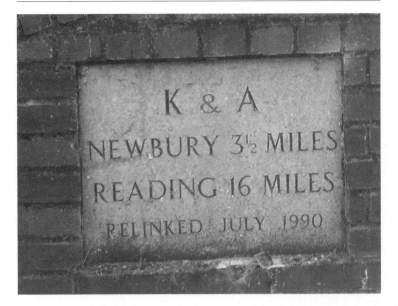

The restoration of the Kennet & Avon Canal was perhaps the greatest restoration triumph.

restoration schemes, but also to core funding. All of a sudden, BW's attempts to achieve self-sufficiency a couple of years earlier began to look prescient. A well-organised campaign was immediately launched, raising the spectre of disused canals and a threat to part of the national heritage, and the old weapon of mass rallies was revived in the last weekend of November 2006.

At the time of writing it is impossible to say whether prognoses of doom and gloom are justified. The budget cuts undoubtedly came as a shock and may well have initiated a period of reflection. Change is a reality of modern life and the waterways were accustomed to it being generally for the good. At the same time, the lobby has already proved itself to be well organised, and as such it is to be hoped that at least it will be able to limit the impact of the cuts and ensure that they do not represent the start of a trend.

This is unlikely. Our canals and rivers are now firmly ensconced in the national psyche with sufficiently interested parties ready to form a coalition to protect them. There is no room for complacency, however, and in the same way that the original pioneers, the Victorians, the bargees, the Number 1s and the Inland Waterways Association all helped make the canals what they are today, now is perhaps the time for the current generation to make their contribution to securing the future.

SECTION K

Taking it easy.

Glossary

Aqueduct	Artificial channel for carrying water
Arm	Offshoot from the main canal
Balance Beam	The protruding arm used to open or shut a lock gate
Barge	A boat of greater than 7ft beam, typically 14ft or more
Beam	Width of a boat
Bollard	Short circular post used for mooring
Bow	Front end of a boat
Broad Canal	Canal with locks capable of taking a barge
Butty	Unpowered boat, usually towed
Caisson	Metal box capable of holding water and boats
Chamber	The part of a lock between the gates
Cill or Sill	Mantle at the back of a lock upon which the upper gate rests
Cruiser	A purpose-made pleasure boat, more usually found on rivers and typically constructed out of wood or fibreglass
Cut	Another term for a canal
Fender	A detachable item used to protect the sides of a boat, usually made from rope, plastic or rubber
Flight	A series of locks close together
Flyboats	A type of lightweight boat that could travel faster than cargo boats and at night
Gate	The (usually wooden) ends of a lock used to hold back water
Gongoozler	Someone who idly watches the progress of boats, usually from a bridge or lock
Guillotine	A vertically raised gate used to block or hold water
Hotel Boats	Narrowboats, usually travelling in pairs, which offer hotel-style holidays on the canals
Inclined Plane	A means of taking boats up the side of a hill, often using rails and pulling the boats up sideways
Legging	A method for taking a boat through a tunnel using human power by walking down the sides
Lift Bridge	Rudimentary type of bridge which lifts to allow traffic to pass
Lock	An enclosure to allow boats to change level
Lockkeeper	Official charged with watching over a lock or series of locks
Lock Key	Alternative name for a windlass
Marina	Site capable of holding a large number of boats, often with associated facilities and a yard
Moorings	Point at which a boat can be secured
Narrowboat	Canal boat with a maximum beam of 7ft and a maximum length of 70ft (60ft on Leeds & Liverpool Canal)
Narrow Canal	Canal built to accommodate narrowboats, defined by having narrow locks
Navvies	Term used to describe original workmen who built the canals – an abbreviation of 'navigators'
Number 1	A boatman who owned his own boat
Outboard	Motor capable of being removed and fitted to the outside of a boat
Packet	Passenger boat
Paddle	Square metal plate used to hold back or allow water into a lock
Pound	Water between two locks
Puddle	Clay mixture which produces a waterproof lining for canals
Pump Out	Vacuum driven system for removing toilet waste from a boat

Reservoir	Large, usually artificial, lakes used to store water to feed a canal
Rudder	A flat structure hinged to the back of a boat to allow it to be steered
Sanitary Station	Location with pump out and other sanitary facilities
Short Boat	Barge only 60ft in length, built for use on the Leeds & Liverpool Canal
Sluice	A gate to control a water channel, usually used in floods
Staircase Locks	Locks built in sequence, with water from one flowing into another, i.e. with no pounds in between
Stoppage	Term used to refer to the temporary closure of a canal, possibly due to a breach or maintenance
Stop Planks	Wood capable of being put into a slot to provide a temporary barrier for water and boats
Summit	The high point of a canal
Swing Bridge	Rudimentary type of bridge which is swung to allow traffic to pass
Tiller	The pole used to turn the rudder
Towpath	The side of a canal defined by the route horses would walk when pulling a boat. Also defines the 'public' side of a canal
Turnover Bridge	Bridge constructed in a way to allow a towing horse to pass from one side of the canal to the other without disconnecting the rope. Sometimes called a roving bridge
Weed Hatch	Detachable opening which allows the clearing of a fouled propeller
Weir	A means of allowing excess water to overflow, usually found alongside locks
Wharf	Place where boats can load or unload their cargoes, usually with a warehouse nearby
Winding	Turning a boat round, the term derives from the original use of the wind to push the boat
Windlass	Cranked handle used to operate lock gear

Learn More and Links

ORGANISATIONS
There is a wealth of information out there available from the various organisations representing different parts of our waterways, with the following amongst the most significant:

Association of Waterways Cruising Clubs – www.awcc.org.uk: focuses on emergency help and overnight moorings for members of affiliated clubs
British Marine Federation – www.britishmarine.co.uk: trade association of the British boating industry
British Waterways – www.britishwaterways.co.uk: responsible for the canals
The Broads Authority – www.broads-authority.gov.uk: responsible for the Broads
The Environment Agency – www.environment-agency.gov.uk: responsible for inland rivers
Inland Waterways Association – www.waterways.org.uk: advocate for securing the future of the waterways
National Association of Boat Owners – www.nabo.org.uk: represents private boat owners
Residential Boat Owners Association – www.rboa.org.uk: represents liveaboard boaters
Royal Yachting Association – www.rya.org.uk: represents pleasure boating
Waterway Recovery Group – www.wrg.org.uk: dedicated to restoring derelict canals.

If you want to know more about the various societies dedicated to restoring our waterways (and in some cases cutting new ones!), there's a useful list on: www.waterways.org.uk/Partners/LocalOrganisations.

WEBSITES
The following is a selection of the many canal-related sites on the web:

www.britishwaterways.co.uk – British Waterways
www.canalia.com – online magazine
www.canaljunction.com – aimed at hirers and owners but goes beyond these
www.canalmedia.co.uk – general resources
www.canals.com – comprehensive site on all things to do with canals
www.jim-shead.co.uk – site for one of the UK's most informed canal advocates
www.justcanals.com – claims to list most canal sites
www.waterscape.com – British Waterways leisure site.

BOOKS
The following is a brief selection of waterways related books. For a more comprehensive list go to: www.iwashop.com.

HISTORY
The Anatomy of Canals: The Early Years – Anthony Burton and Derek Pratt (Tempus Publishing, 2001)
The Anatomy of Canals: Mania Years – Anthony Burton and Derek Pratt (Tempus Publishing, 2002)
The Anatomy of Canals: Decline and Renewal – Anthony Burton and Derek Pratt (Tempus Publishing, 2003)
James Brindley: The First Canal Builder – Nick Corble (Tempus Publishing, 2005)

The Canal Builders – Anthony Burton (Tempus Publishing, 2005)
Hadfield's British Canals – (Sutton Publishing, 1998)
Waterways in the Making – Edward Paget-Tomlinson (Landscape Press, 1996)

GENERAL
Canal Boats and Barges – Tony Condor (Shire Books 2004)
Colours of the Cut – Edward Paget-Tomlinson, A. Lewery (Landscape Press, 2004)
Wildlife of Rivers and Canals – Tony Hopkins and Pat Brassley (Morland Pub. Co., 1982)

GUIDES AND WALKING
Nicholson's Guides to the Waterways – (Nicholson's, various)
Pearson's Canal Companions – (Pearsons, various)
Tempus Towpath Guides – Nick Corble (Tempus Publishing, various)
Walking Britain's Canals and Rivers – Paul Atterbury and David Bellamy (Harper Collins, 1999)
Waterside Walks series – (Countryside Books, various)

TRAVELOGUES
Athene: Anatomy of a Dream – Anthony Lewis (Athene Books, 1997)
Narrow Boat – L.T.C. Rolt (Sutton Publishing, 1994)
Paddling to Jerusalem – David Aaronovich (Fourth Estate, 2000)
Walking on Water – Nick Corble (Belmont Press 2007)
The Water Road – Paul Gogarty (Robson Books, 2003)
The Worst Journey in the Midlands – Sam Llewellyn (Summersdale Publishers, 2003)

PRACTICALITIES
Canal and River Cruising: The IWA Manual – Sheila Davenport (Fernhurst Books, 1998)
The Inland Boat Owners Book – Andrew Burnett (Waterways World, 2000)
Inland Cruising: Practical Course Notes – (Royal Yachting Association, 1995)
The Inland Waterways Manual – Emrhys Barrell (Adlard Coles Nautical, 2001)
The Liveaboard Report: A Boat Dweller's Guide to What Works and What Doesn't (McGraw-Hill Publishing, 1993)
The Narrowboat Builder's Book – Graham Booth and Andrew Burnett (Waterways World 1995)
Narrow Boats Care and Maintenance – Nick Billingham (Helmsman Books, 1995)
Simple Boat Electrics – John Myatt (Fernhurst Books, 1997)
Simple Boat Maintenance – Pat Manley (Fernhurst Books, 2005)

FICTION
Death in Little Venice – Leo McNair (Enigma Publishing, 2001) – one of many books by this author with a waterways theme
Greasy Ocker – Derek Pratt (Enigma Publishing, 2005)
The Narrowboat Girl – Annie Murray (Pan, 2001) – one of many books by this author with a waterways theme
The Rose Revived – Katie Fforde (Arrow, 2003) – one of many books by this author with a waterways theme
Three Men In A Boat – Jerome K. Jerome (Penguin Classic, 1994)
The Wench is Dead – Colin Dexter (Pan, 1991)

Index

If you are interested in purchasing other books published by Tempus, or in case you have difficulty finding any Tempus books in your local bookshop, you can also place orders directly through our website

www.tempus-publishing.com